PORSCHE

VORWORT

Schottland gehört nicht gerade zu den Glamour-Destinationen dieser Welt. Weit abgelegen, furchtbar schwer zu erreichen, mit einer Wetterprognose, an der nur ihre Wechselhaftigkeit vorhersehbar ist. Und trotzdem ist da dieser Reiz des Ursprünglichen und Rauen, der gerade Freunde des Soulful Driving unerbittlich anzieht. Die schottischen Highlands sind CURVES pur – nicht wegen einer kompromisslos hohen Kurven-zu-Gesamtkilometer-Ratio, sondern weil hier die Magie stimmt. Weil dramatische Landschaft und Fahrdynamik-Sog eine intensive Verbindung eingehen, die bereits nach wenigen Meilen hypnotischen Suchtcharakter entfaltet. Schottland ist ein zwingender Kandidat für CURVES. *Soulful Driving. Los geht's.*

—

Scotland is not exactly one of the most glamorous destinations in the world. It's isolated, terribly difficult to reach, and has weather that can only be forecast as changeable. Yet, there is a certain charm in its authenticity and ruggedness, a charm that has an irresistible pull, particularly on friends of soulful driving. The Scottish Highlands are quintessential CURVES – not because of an uncompromisingly high corner-to-total-miles ratio, but because this is where magic lives. Because dramatic landscapes and the pull of driving dynamics form an intense bond that evolves into a hypnotically additive character after just a few miles. Scotland is a compelling candidate for CURVES. *For soulful driving. Let's go.*

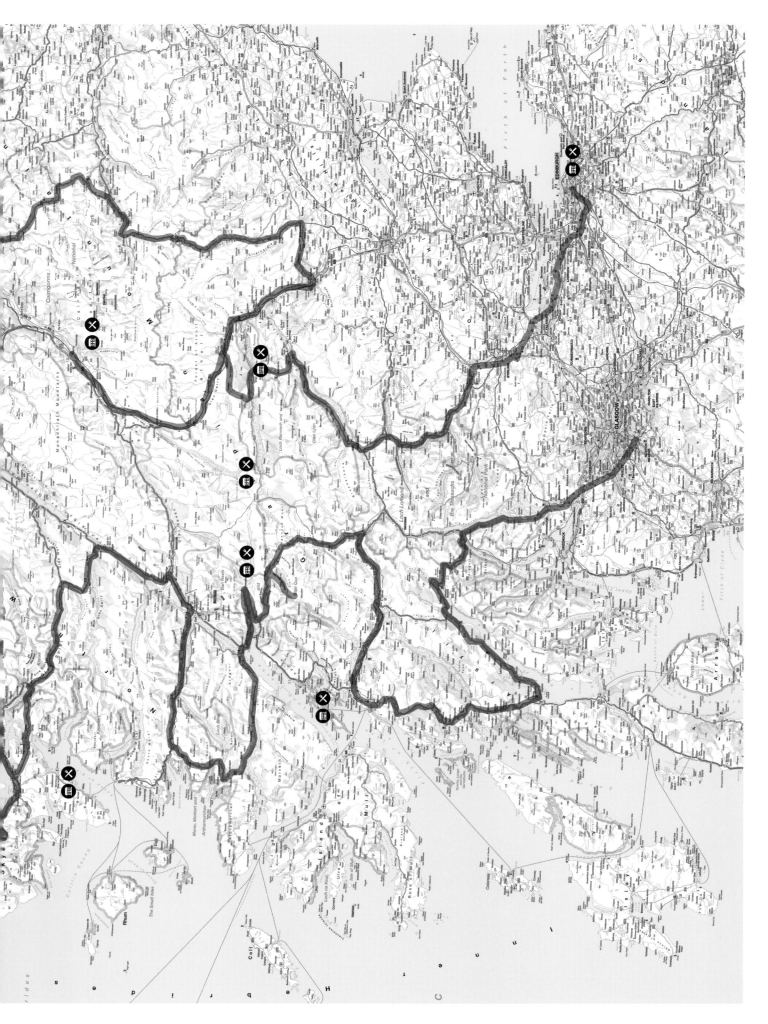

Glasgow ist kein wirklich beschwingter Einstieg in unsere Schottland-Reise, aber eine Stadt mit Gewicht, die einen gleich in die verwegene, raue Atmosphäre Schottlands zieht. Mit der ersten Tour-Etappe durch den Nationalpark „Loch Lomond and The Trossachs" zeigt sich Schottland noch von seiner eher lieblichen Seite, auch der erste Abstecher ans Meer hat noch weiche Züge für Liebhaber von Natur und Einsamkeit. Spätestens auf der Fahrt übers Rannoch Moor sind wir allerdings im Schottland für Fortgeschrittene angekommen. Die Weite dieser beinahe menschenfeindlichen Landschaft und ihre bedrohliche Schönheit ziehen einen in ihren magischen Bann, touristische Leichtigkeit oder angenehmes Meilenfressen darf hier nicht erwartet werden. Auch auf der Schlussetappe in Richtung Isle of Skye herrscht die verwunschene Stimmung eines Troll-Thrillers – genau dafür sind wir aber nach Schottland gekommen.

Glasgow is not a particularly exciting gateway to our Scotland journey, but it's a city with gravitas, one that pulls you right into the audacious, rugged atmosphere of Scotland. With the first stage of the trip through the national parks of Loch Lomond and The Trossachs, Scotland displays its somewhat gentler side, and the first stretch along the ocean offers softer features for admirers of nature and solitude. But once we reach the Great Moor of Rannoch, we've arrived in Scotland for the advanced. The vastness of this almost hostile landscape and its ominous beauty cast a magical spell, but don't expect an easy Sunday outing or mile upon mile of driving pleasure. And even the final leg towards the Isle of Skye is dominated by the haunted mood of a troll thriller – but that's precisely why we have come to Scotland.

Anfahrt über die kleine Fähre von Glenelg nach Kylerhea, dann nach Norden: Wer die rund 200 Kilometer lange Etappe über die Isle of Skye nonstop durchfährt, dürfte dafür rund vier Stunden brauchen – allerdings ist das hier kaum zu erwarten. Im Wesentlichen verläuft die Route über schmale Single Track Roads, auf denen höchste Vorsicht und moderates Tempo angesagt sind. Nicht selten tauchen entgegenkommende Fahrzeuge erst im letzten Moment hinter einem Felsbrocken oder aus kaum wahrnehmbaren Bodensenken auf, hinzu kommen halbwilde Schafe, die plötzlich mitten auf der Fahrbahn stehen. Abgesehen von diesen Sicherheitshinweisen bremst die Isle of Skye aber vor allem durch ihre Schönheit: Von lieblich bis schroff verführt eine sagenhafte Landschaft mit eigentümlich ruhiger Atmosphäre zum Anhalten und Umsehen. Erst die wilde, abenteuerliche und umwerfend dramatische Passstraße am Quiraing lässt einen in hechelnden CURVES-Modus verfallen. Am Ende des Tages hat man sich dann auch die bequeme Fahrt aufs Festland über die Brücke bei Kyle of Lochalsh mehr als verdient.

Take the small ferry from Glenelg to Kylerhea, then head north. The entire 200 kilometres around the Isle of Skye in one go take about four hours – but this is unrealistic. Essentially, the route runs over narrow one-lane roads which require utmost caution and moderate speeds. Not infrequently, oncoming vehicles appear suddenly from behind a boulder or from barely perceptible hollows, added to this are the semi-wild sheep that often like to stand in the middle of the road. Apart from these cautionary tips, the excursion around the Isle of Skye is slow thanks to its beauty: from charming to rugged, this stunning landscape seduces travellers to linger and soak in its strangely tranquil atmosphere. Finally, in true CURVES manner, the wild, adventurous and breathtakingly dramatic pass road at Quiraing leaves us panting breathlessly. At the end of the day, the pleasant drive to the mainland over the bridge at Kyle of Lochalsh is well-earned.

**ETAPPE
STAGE**

**ETAPPE
STAGE**

Mit einem Besuch des Eilean Donan Castle starten wir historisch und touristisch hochwertig in die dritte Tagesetappe, danach geht es weiter in nördlicher Richtung zur Applecross-Halbinsel. Der sogenannte Bealach na Bà, also „Vieh-Pass", wurde nach den Viehtreibern früherer Jahrhunderte benannt, war einmal der einzige Weg zur Westseite der Insel und ist noch immer ein fahrerisches Sahnestück. Wer nicht über den Pass und wieder zurück fahren möchte, kann heutzutage eine Rundfahrt um die gesamte Halbinsel unternehmen: von Lochcarron kommend über den Pass nach Applecross, weiter zum Loch Shieldaig und am Torridon-Massiv wieder zurück nach Süden. Es empfiehlt sich jedoch eine Fahrt im Uhrzeigersinn, da das extreme Gefälle am Bealach na Bà harmonischer als Bergauf-Passage genommen wird. Wir folgen nach unserer Tour über die Halbinsel dem Verlauf der Westküste bis nach Ullapool und schließen dort die dritte Etappe ab.

Die Westküste des schottischen Festlands ähnelt mit ihren tief ins Land geschnittenen Buchten und Fjords, den Bergen und der geröllbedeckten Landschaft an vielen Stellen ihrer skandinavischen Nachbarschaft im Osten. Dass die frühe Geschichte Schottlands darüber hinaus immer wieder durch Besiedlung aus Skandinavien geprägt wurde, ist an vielen Ortsnamen und regionalen Geschichten abzulesen – es macht große Freude, bei der Fahrt zum nördlichen Ende Großbritanniens diese Ahnungen und Andeutungen einzusammeln. Von Ullapool aus entfernen wir uns aber zuerst vom Atlantik und fahren bis Unapool durchs Inland. Dann folgen wir der Küstenlinie bis Scourie und ziehen dort eine Gerade nach Durness an der Nordküste. Von hier aus geht es einige Meilen in Richtung Osten, dann beginnt der lange Weg über die Südspitze des Loch Shin bis nach Inverness, der eindeutig größten Stadt des nördlichen Schottland.

We start the tour of day three with a worthwhile historic and touristy visit to Eilean Donan Castle before heading north towards the Applecross peninsula. The so-called Bealach na Bà, or pass of the cattle, was historically used as a drover's road, it was the only route to the west side of the island and is a motorist's paradise. Nowadays, those who would prefer not to make the return trip over the pass can take the route around the entire peninsula: From Lochcarron over the pass to Applecross, on to Loch Shieldaig and at the Torridon massif back to the south. The recommendation is to drive in a clockwise direction, since the extreme downhill gradient at Bealach na Bà is more harmonious than the uphill passage. After our tour around the peninsula, we continue along the west coast to Ullapool and that concludes the third leg.

Many places along the west coast of the Scottish mainland, with its bays and fjords cutting deep inland and scree-sloped mountains, resemble its Scandinavian neighbours in the east. Indeed, the early history of Scotland has always been characterised by settlers from Scandinavia and this can be seen by the many local names and regional stories. It's a great joy to drive to the northern tip of Great Britain and learn about these morsels. From Ullapool we say goodbye for the time being to the Atlantic. We pop inland to Unapool and out again along the coastline to Scourie. From there it's straight ahead to Durness and the north coast. We drive several miles to the east from here before beginning the long journey over the southern tip of Loch Shin to Inverness, definitely the largest city in northern Scotland.

5

**ETAPPE
STAGE**

Dem überaus lieblichen Küstenabschnitt östlich von
Inverness mit seinen flachen Sandstränden folgen wir
nur für wenige Meilen, dann zieht es uns nach Süden zum
3800 Quadratkilometer großen Cairngorms Nationalpark.
Durch den nahezu menschenleeren und erst seit 2003
geschützten Park führen nur wenige Straßen. Das Land
rund um die bis über 1300 Meter hohen Grampian Mountains entfaltet einen ganz eigenen Charakter, weitläufig,
intensiv und freundlich. Nach einem Besuch im spektakulären Balmoral Castle folgen wir den großen Hauptverkehrsstraßen im Osten Schottlands bis nach Edinburgh.
Die schottische Hauptstadt am Firth of Forth mit ihren
rund 500 000 Einwohnern ist das Ziel der letzten Etappe
und unserer Schottland-Rundfahrt.

We only follow the exceptionally picturesque coastal
section east of Inverness with its flat sand beaches for a
few miles before heading south to the 3,800-square-kilo-
metre Cairngorms National Park. Only a few roads run
through the almost uninhabited park, which was only put
under protection in 2003. The land around the 1,300-metre-
high Grampian Mountains reveals its own character:
expansive, intense and welcoming. After a visit to the
spectacular Balmoral Castle we follow the major roads
to eastern Scotland and on to Edinburgh. The Scottish
capital with around half a million inhabitants on the
Firth of Forth is the destination of the last leg of our
round-trip of Scotland.

INTRO

Ein Land am Ende der Welt, ein Land voller Geschichten und Geheimnisse: Aus der Perspektive des Reisenden ist Schottland eine Mischung aus uneinlösbarem Traum und beinahe schmerzhaftem Sehnsuchtsort. Diese exponierte Lage im Herzen aller Fernweh-Junkies verdankt Schottland vor allem seiner sowohl gefühlten als auch realen Distanz zu allen anderen Orten der Welt. Beinahe überall auf unserem Globus befindet man sich zwischen zwei Punkten, zwischen Heimat und Unbekanntem, zwischen Nah und Fern – Schottland liegt aber auf dem Weg nach Nirgendwo. Nordatlantik, Ende. Nicht einmal auf dem Weg nach Island oder Nordamerika würde man einen Zwischenstopp in Schottland einlegen, das Land ist eine Sackgasse. Danach kommt einfach nichts mehr und deshalb muss Schottland selbst das Ziel sein. Grau, karg, windgepeitscht, von Menschen bevölkert, die als geizig, streitsüchtig und eigenwillig gelten. Das Essen soll schlecht sein, die Lochs abgrundtief, die Ungeheuer riesig und das Wetter miserabel. Weshalb also Schottland?

Vielleicht ja gerade deshalb: Weil man sich dieses Land ganz bewusst vorenthält und dann zumutet, weil man hier nicht einfach mal vorbeikommt und Schottland deshalb Reisen für Fortgeschrittene bedeutet. Und wen dieser bildungsbürgerlich-philosophische Ansatz nicht kitzelt, den lockt vielleicht das Abenteuer, das Andere, Ursprüngliche und Unerklärliche. Auch wenn diese gefühlige Schwärmerei für ein sagenumwobenes Land im Norden vielleicht nur ganz wenig mit der Realität Schottlands zu tun hat. Erklärungsversuch: Wir alle leben in einer Welt, die vom Geist des römischen Imperiums durchdrungen ist, unsere Sprache, unsere Wissenschaft, unsere Maßeinheiten, unsere Technologie, unsere Ordnung, unsere Politik, unser Militär, unsere Zivilisation, unsere Religion – kurz gefasst: Unsere gesamte Art zu denken ist auch rund 1500 Jahre später immer noch schockierend intensiv von einem guten Jahrtausend römischer Herrschaft über Europa

A country at the end of the world, a land packed with stories and secrets: From a traveller's perspective, Scotland is a combination of unfulfillable dreams and an almost painful place of longing. This exposed location in the heart of all wanderlust junkies is by and large due to Scotland's perceived and real distance to every other place in the world. Almost everywhere on our planet you find yourself between two points, between home and the unknown, between near and far – Scotland, however, lies on the road to nowhere. North Atlantic, end. Scotland isn't even a stopover en route to Iceland or North America, the country is a cul-de-sac. After that there's simply nothing, hence Scotland alone has to be the destination. Grey, barren, windswept and inhabited by people who are regarded as tight-fisted, belligerent and headstrong. The food is supposed to be dreadful, the lochs abysmal, the monsters huge, the weather miserable. So why Scotland?

Perhaps that's exactly the reason: Because people very deliberately sidestep this country but then decide to risk it, because you can't just pop in, and this makes Scotland a travel destination for the advanced. And if this bourgeois-philosophical approach doesn't tickle the fancy, then perhaps the adventure, the something else, the authentic, the unexplainable, just might. Even if this sentimental gushing for a legend-shrouded country in the north may have little to do with the reality of Scotland. An attempt to explain: We all live in a world that is imbued with the spirit of the Roman Empire, our language, our science, our units of measurement, our technology, our law and order, our politics, our military, our civilisation, our religion – in short, our entire way of thinking, around 1,500 years of it is still influenced to a shocking degree by a good millennium of Roman rule over Europe and the Mediterranean realm. In this subconscious coordinate system, Scotland is still this mysterious territory beyond the familiar. What happened north of the Hadrian's Wall has fed myths and

Danach kommt einfach nichts mehr und deshalb muss Schottland selbst das Ziel sein. Grau, karg, windgepeitscht, von Menschen bevölkert, die als geizig, streitsüchtig und eigenwillig gelten.

After that there's simply nothing, hence Scotland alone has to be the destination. Grey, barren, windswept and inhabited by people who are regarded as tight-fisted, belligerent and headstrong.

und den Mittelmeer-Raum geprägt. In diesem unterbewussten Koordinatensystem ist Schottland nach wie vor diese geheimnisvolle Gegend jenseits des Bekannten. Was dort nördlich des Hadrianswalls passierte, hat jahrhundertelang Mythen gefüttert und Vorurteile genährt, ohne je eine Chance auf Klarstellung gehabt zu haben. Unser Schottland-Bild ist also verzerrt, weil bereits die Brille nicht stimmt, durch die wir den Norden Großbritanniens sehen.

Ein naives Kind in uns überzieht das Bild von Schottland mit dem Zuckerguss von Sehnsucht nach Rauheit, Echtheit und Heidentum, will das wilde Land eins sehen mit dem ungebeugten Freiheitsdrang der „Kelten" (zu denen die Schotten in unserer süßlichen Verklärung kurzerhand werden), möchte etwas wahr- und liebhaben, das in unserer abgebrühten Zivilisation längst verloren scheint – und übersieht dafür gerne das wahre Schottland. Unterwegs in den Norden der britischen Insel empfiehlt es sich also, ein paar Minuten für die Geschichte Schottlands zu investieren. Clan-Kriege, William Wallace, Mary Stuart und so weiter. Klassischer Realitätscheck. Sie wollen jetzt schon wissen, wie es ausgeht? Nur so viel: Heutige Schotten tragen ganze gerne mal einen Slip unterm Kilt ...

Übrig bleibt das Land. Knapp 80 000 Quadratkilometer, die sich schon rein geologisch mit England schwertun: Als erdgeschichtliche Landdrift hat sich der Felsbrocken, den wir heute Schottland nennen, vor zig Millionen Jahren irgendwo in Nordamerika losgezappelt, Kurs auf (das was heute) Europa (ist) genommen und dabei zufällig England gerammt. Liebesgeschichten gehen irgendwie anders. All der geologische Stress hat jedenfalls dafür gesorgt, dass Schottland seine Highlands hat – die ehemals bis auf 8000er-Niveau aufgefaltete Gebirgsgegend ist heute immer noch sagenhaft schroff, Eiszeit-Gletscher haben allerdings für Nivellierung gesorgt. Als höchster Berg Schottlands und Gesamt-Großbritanniens ist der Ben Nevis nur noch 1345 Meter hoch. Der Reiz der schottischen

cultivated prejudices for centuries without ever having a chance of clarification. Our idea of Scotland is distorted because the glasses through which we view the north of Great Britain have been warped.

The naive child in us overlays the image of Scotland with an icing of longing for ruggedness, authenticity and paganism, it wants to see the wild country at one with the Celt's (who we like to make the Scots in our dreams) tenacious desire for independence, the child wants to believe and hold dear a certain something that our hard-nosed civilisation seems to have lost long ago, and blithely ignores the real Scotland. When travelling through the north of the British Isles it pays to spend a few minutes investing in the history of Scotland. Clan feuds, William Wallace, Mary Stuart and so on. A classic reality check. Do you want to know how it all ends? We'll give you this much: Scotsmen of today prefer to wear boxers under their kilts...

What's left is the land. Almost 80,000 square kilometres that, from a purely geological point of view, has it tough with England: As a geological continental drift, the lump of rock that we call Scotland today flailed its way from somewhere in North America umpteen million years ago and headed for (what is now) Europe and accidentally rammed into England. Love stories go somewhat differently. All that geological stress, however, gave Scotland its Highlands – a mountain range, which at one point had hoisted itself up to 8,000 metres, that is still

Highlands liegt allerdings nicht in ihrer Höhe, sondern in ihrer Textur: tiefe und lange Täler, die jeden Verkehr in ihren Wuchsrhythmus zwingen, ein feuchtes Klima aus Atlantik und Golfstrom, das für üppige Vegetation sowie mit Wasser vollgesogene Moore sorgt – und natürlich die Lochs. Seen in allen Größenordnungen, von Tümpel-klein bis Fjord-riesig. Die Highlands sind eine Gegend von gefühlter Unendlichkeit und großer Zeitlosigkeit. Wer hier stundenlang für wenige Kilometer braucht, während er über winzige Straßen streunt, die ihren Ursprung in alten Clan-Pfaden haben, fühlt sich regelrecht verschluckt von dieser mächtigen Landschaft unter einem turbulenten Himmel.

Sowieso, die Straßen … Da haben wir sie ja wieder, unsere Romanisierung: Die großen Straßen Europas verlaufen immer noch auf den alten Trassen der Römer; wir haben uns an die entfernungsverachtende Dreistigkeit gewöhnt, mit der sie als Effizienz-Instrument einer kühlen Verwaltung auf möglichst funktionalen Routen durchs Land schneiden. Im Land der Barbaren gibt es das nicht. Schottische Straßen sind lokal. Sie schmiegen sich ganz organisch an Berghänge und schlängeln sich durch Täler, man spürt ihnen ab, dass sie nicht vom Straßenbauer auf einem Blatt Papier geplant, sondern von Füßen und Hufen ins Land getreten wurden. Sobald man sich an ihren kleinteiligen Rhythmus gewöhnt hat, wie sie von Brücke zu Brücke, von Hügel zu Hügel, von Loch zu Loch schwingen, verfällt man ihnen restlos. In ihrer Selbstverständlichkeit liegt eine wunderliche Schönheit, die einen dazu zwingt, in ebenso überschaubaren Etappen zu denken. Gewaltige Tagestouren, wie sie auf US-amerikanischen Highways oder deutschen Autobahnen machbar sind, werden in Schottland unwirklich und unnötig. Denn auf einmal beginnt das Land Geschichten zu erzählen, die jeden in ihren Bann ziehen.

Weshalb also Schottland? Weil man in den meisten Gegenden dieser Welt ausgezeichnet unterwegs sein kann, im Sog der Reise aber nur selten ankommt. In Schottland ist das genau andersherum. Hier ist überall das Ziel.

GLENCOE

incredibly rugged today, but ice age glaciers have taken the edges off. At 1,345 metres, Ben Nevis is Scotland's highest mountain, the highest in all of Great Britain, in fact. The appeal of the Scottish Highlands, however, is not due to height but texture: Deep and long valleys, forcing all traffic to adhere to their growth pattern, a humid climate from the Atlantic and the Gulf Stream which cultivates lush vegetation and water-filled moors – and of course lochs. Lakes of all sizes, from wee ponds to giant fjords. The Highlands is a region of perceived endlessness and great timelessness. Those who spend hours for just a few kilometres while meandering over the tiny streets with their origins in ancient clan trails, feel completely consumed by this mighty landscape under a turbulent sky.

And the roads are no different. And there it is again, our Romanisation: The great roads of Europe still follow the old marked-out routes of the Romans. We've become accustomed to the distance-defying audacity with which they cut through the land as efficient instruments of a detached administration on routes as functional as possible. There's none of that in the land of the barbarians. Scotland's roads are local. They hug the mountain slopes very naturally and snake through valleys, it's easy to see that they have not been planned on a drawing board by engineers but are tromped into the countryside by feet and hooves. As soon as you become accustomed to the small-scale rhythm, how they flow from bridge to bridge, from hill to hill, from loch to loch, you'll fall completely in love with them. In their implicitness lies a wondrous beauty, compelling you to also think in manageable legs: massive daily distances, as is possible on US highways or German autobahns, are simply unrealistic and unnecessary in Scotland. For all of a sudden the country begins to tell stories that enthral one and all.

So, why Scotland? Because we can travel excellently through most regions of the world, but the momentum of the journey rarely allows you to "arrive". In Scotland it's the other way round. Here, the destination is everywhere.

EILEAN DONAN
CASTLE

QUIRAING PASS

SKYFALL

GLASGOW
ISLE OF SKYE

656 KM • 11 STUNDEN // 407 MILES • 11 HOURS

Glasgow ist der Anfang unserer Reise, aber nicht der Anfang von Schottland: Wer mit dem Auto vom europäischen Festland kommt, dürfte in den allermeisten Fällen zuerst das blutige Opfer einer langen Fahrt durch England auf dem Altar der Reiselust dargebracht haben. Über oder unter den Ärmelkanal, dann entlang der Londoner Ringautobahn, die sich in manchen Tageszeiten zum größten Parkplatz Europas verwandelt.

—

Glasgow is the beginning of our journey, but it's not the beginning of Scotland: Travellers who arrive by car from the European continent will probably have to endure a long pilgrimage through England to reach the altar of wanderlust. First, above or below the English Channel, crawling around London's M25 ring road, which can at times turn into Europe's largest car park.

INVERARAY CASTLE

INVERARAY PA32 8XE
TEL.: +44 1499 3022033
WWW.INVERARAY-CASTLE.COM

Weiter über die M6 nach Norden, stundenlang, vorbei an Birmingham, immer weiter, zwischen Manchester und Liverpool der englischen Westküste entgegen. Die Aggregatzustände der Naturgewalt „Verkehrsstau" sind auf diesen vielen hundert Meilen beinahe so vielfältig wie die Nuancen des englischen Wetters. Reisende haben reelle Chancen, alles von strahlendem Sonnenschein bis hin zu triefendem Regen innerhalb eines halben Tages zu erleben. Irgendwann wünscht man sich, den Traum von Schottland auf die sanfte Tour per Flugzeug eingefädelt zu haben – aber hey, CURVES im vierzylindrig-dieselnden Mietwagen? No way!

Hinter Lancaster reicht der Norden dann endlich seine moosige, steinerne Hand zu einem ersten Willkommensgruß. Von Null auf Magie in unter drei Sekunden – die einsamen Berge des Lake District sind eine Szenerie, die einen fast von der Weiterfahrt abhält. Penrith, Carlisle, dann endlich die Grenze nach Schottland. Bis nach Glasgow sind es dann aber immer noch 140 Kilometer durch die Lowlands, und dann endlich ist alles anders. Wir haben das Tor nach Schottland aufgestoßen. Mühsam, unermüdlich, mit den Schultern eines Riesen, aber jetzt sind wir tatsächlich hier. Geschwärzte Mauern aus grauem Stein, graue Straßen, grauer Himmel, dazu der dunkle Herzschlag einer alten, müden Arbeiterstadt: Glasgow, die Stadt am Clyde, stolpert einer unruhigen Zukunft entgegen. Ohne Werften, Kohle und Schwerindustrie haben es die fast 2 Millionen Glaswegians schwer im steifen Gegenwind der Globalisierung. Alkoholismus und Kriminalität sind Begleiterscheinungen einer lang anhaltenden Identitätskrise – und trotzdem stemmt sich Glasgow stoisch gegen den Abstieg. Der Stolz einer Stadt kann sich einigeln, in den Untergrund gehen und sonderbar bunte Blüten treiben. Dieses Phänomen teilt Glasgow mit in den Wandel gezwungenen Städten wie Detroit/Michigan oder dem deutschen Ruhrgebiet. Glasgow war nie lieblich oder angenehm und wird es wohl nie werden, aber als Startpunkt einer Reise ans Ende der Welt taugt es regelrecht ideal.

For hours on end, we follow the M6 to the north, leaving Birmingham behind. Past Manchester and Liverpool to the left and right, we continue ever onwards parallel to the west coast of England. Over these many hundreds of miles, traffic jams are a force of nature and come in many state of matter, almost as diverse as the nuances of British weather. Travellers have a reasonable chance of experiencing bright sunshine followed by torrential downpours within half a day. At times, the dream of reaching Scotland in the rarefied air of a modern aircraft seems so much more appealing – but hey, CURVES in a four-cylinder diesel-powered rental car? No way!

After Lancaster, the North finally extends its stony, moss-covered hand as a welcome, from zero to magic in less than three seconds. The lonesome mountains of the Lake District offer a backdrop that almost stops us in our tracks. Penrith, Carlisle, then finally the Scottish border. There're still 140 kilometres to Glasgow through the Lowlands, but then, at last, everything changes. We've pushed open the gates to Scotland. Unswervingly, with determination and shoulder to the wheel, we've finally arrived. Blackened walls of grey rock, grey roads, grey skies and the dark heartbeat of an old, tired industrial city: Glasgow, the city on the Clyde, stumbles towards an uncertain future. Without shipyards, coal and heavy industries, the two million or so Glaswegians have a hard time facing the stiff headwind of globalisation. Alcoholism and crime are the side effects of a long-standing identity crisis – and yet Glasgow stoically stems the tide of its downfall. The pride of a city can curl up in a ball, go underground and send out incredibly beautiful blossoms, a phenomenon that Glasgow shares with other cities that have been forced into change, such as Detroit/Michigan or Germany's Ruhr region. Glasgow was never particularly lovely or pleasant and it never will be, but it's an ideal starting point for a journey to the end of the world. At the mouth of the many-limbed Firth of Clyde we cross a slow-moving, almost inky stretch

Glasgow war nie lieblich oder angenehm und wird es wohl nie werden, aber als Startpunkt einer Reise ans Ende der Welt taugt es regelrecht ideal.

Glasgow was never particularly lovely or pleasant and it never will be, but it's an ideal starting point for a journey to the end of the world.

An der Mündung in die verästelte Firth of Clyde überqueren wir das träge, nahezu schwarz wirkende Band des Flusses Clyde in imposanter Höhe; die moderne Hängeseilbrücke wird zum Wurmloch in ein anderes Universum. Wir landen auf der A82 in Richtung Nordwesten. Kurz geht es noch für wenige Meilen durch die letzten Ausläufer der Zivilisation, dann wird die Welt grün, saftig und verwunschen. Der Verkehr der Stadt und ihrer Randgebiete versickert zu einem spärlichen Rinnsal, die Straße ist grob und feucht. Sonnenstrahlen flackern durch die Bäume am Ufer des Loch Lomond und nur die niedrige Steinmauer zwischen Asphaltband und Seeufer scheint diese wild sprießende Vegetation davon abzuhalten, auch die Straße zu überwuchern. Am Nordostende des Sees macht sich die knapp 980 Meter hohe Kuppe des Ben Lomond breit, für uns geht es jetzt am gegenüberliegenden Seeufer auf die A83 zum Loch Long und dann weiter zum Loch Fyne. Hier zeigt Schottland seine atmosphärische Verwandtschaft mit Skandinavien: Der über 60 Kilometer lange Fjord mit seinen tangbedeckten Kiesstränden wirkt ebenso endlos und unterkühlt wie die Meeresarme in Norwegen.

Wir setzen uns auf einen bröckelnden Bootsanleger aus Beton und schnuppern die würzige Luft, inhalieren eine Mischung aus Wald, Moos und Meerwasserduft. Möwen stürzen sich in waghalsigen Pirouetten über den Himmel und balgen sich um eine imaginäre Lufthoheit oder hocken wie festgefroren auf großen Felsblöcken. Der immer wieder vom Atlantik her wiederkehrende Regen fließt über die umliegenden Berge zurück in den Fjord, verdünnt das Salz des Meeres und sorgt so für wimmelndes Leben im Wasser. Plankton, Krebse, Muscheln. Robben und Delphine sind hier oben unterwegs, und während des kurzen Sommers soll sich sogar hin und wieder einer der gigantischen Riesenhaie in den Loch verirren. Ein paar Schritte entfernt laden Fischer Austern in einen Kleintransporter, mit etwas Glück gibt es die beinahe süßlich schmeckenden Muscheln frisch geöffnet auf die Hand und die Jungs erzählen nuschelnd Seemannsgarn: Beinahe zehn

of the Clyde River at an imposing height, the modern suspension bridge becomes the wormhole into another world. We find ourselves on the A82 heading northwest.

We drive through the last few straggling foothills of civilisation before the world turns green – luscious and enchanting. The traffic of the city and its outer suburbs evaporates into a sparse trickle, the road surface becomes rough and damp. Sunlight filters through trees at the shores of Loch Lomond and only the low stone wall separating the strip of asphalt and the riverbank seems to stop this wildly sprouting vegetation from smothering the road. At the northeast end of the lake towers the 980-metre peak of Ben Lomond. We now cross to the other side of the lake onto the A83 to Loch Long and further to Loch Fyne. The mood in this part of Scotland is a lot like Scandinavia, the 60-kilometre-long fjord with its seaweed-littered pebbly beaches as endless and chilly as Norway's inlets.

We sit on a crumbling concrete boat dock and sniff the tangy air, a heady brew of forest, moss and saltwater. Seagulls wheel in daring pirouettes above us, scrapping amongst themselves for imaginary air supremacy or perching as if frozen on boulders. Rain sweeps in curtains across the Atlantic, the deluge flows from the surrounding mountains into the lochs, mingling with seawater and creating a bouillabaisse teeming with sealife. Plankton, crabs, shellfish. Here, seals and dolphins cavort, and during the short summers sometimes even gigantic basking sharks lose their way in the loch. Nearby, fishermen load oysters into a van. With a little luck, the sweet mussels are prised open and the sailors share some yarns: Sharks almost ten metres long, they said, with enormous caudal fins – enough to make your blood freeze. Grinning impishly, while tossing the slurped-empty oyster shells into the water, they explain: Basking sharks feed on plankton, they glide through the water with mouths stretched wide and filter their diminutive catch. Still, for us

LOCH BA

LOCH BA

GLENCOE MOUNTAINS

Meter lang sollen die Haie sein, mit einer enormen Rückenflosse ausgestattet und bei Zufallsbegegnungen für eiskalt gerinnendes Blut sorgen. Lauerndes Grinsen, die leergeschlürften Austernschalen fliegen mit einer schnellen Bewegung weggeschleudert ins Wasser, dann folgt die Aufklärung: Riesenhaie sind Planktonfresser, die mit weit aufgerissenem Maul durchs Wasser ziehen und sich so den Magen mit Kleinstgetier füllen. Die Vorstellung, draußen auf dem dunklen Meeresarm plötzlich so einem Riesen zu begegnen, bleibt für uns Landratten trotzdem ein wenig beunruhigend. Zurück ins Auto. Legenden sammeln.

Wie ein Spiegel liegt die Wasseroberfläche des Loch Fyne da, wir folgen der Straße an seinem Nordufer entlang und landen kurz vor Inveraray auf einer alten Steinbrücke, die den hier im Fjord mündenden River Aray überquert. Hübsch zelebriertes Drama mit einspuriger Ampelregelung – auf dem Brückenbogen dann großes „Oh" und „Ah": Wie mit dem Riesenrasenmäher in die Uferwiesen eingefräst zieht sich sattgrüner Rasen den Hügel hinauf und öffnet so den Blick auf Inveraray Castle. Der Stammsitz des Duke of Argyll kauert mit seinen graugrünen Mauern und mächtigen Rundtürmen samt spitzen Dachkegeln an allen vier Ecken wie ein im Mittelalter gelandetes Raumschiff in der Landschaft, der Übergang zwischen umgebender Wildnis und mit der Nagelschere getrimmtem Schlossgarten ist kaum wahrzunehmen. Rechtsschwenk, Schlossbesichtigung. Eintauchen ins Wesen und Unwesen des Campbell-Clans, hochdosierte schottische Geschichte, alle Mythen- und Traumspeicher werden bei so einer Gelegenheit randvoll getankt. Hinter Inveraray zieht sich die A819 durchs Flusstal des Aray, leichte Bögen, griffiger Asphalt und in den Fluss-Auen aus einem blauen Himmel strahlende Sonne machen die Fahrt zu einem Ereignis: Obwohl wir uns am Ende beinahe exakt in Richtung Norden zum Loch Awe bei Cladich bewegt haben, ist auf diesen 15 Kilometern keine einzige Gerade zu finden. Stattdessen langgezogene Wechselkurven, von Birken gesäumt, die grünen Hügel dahinter scheinen endlos vorüberzuziehen. Dann geht es hinter der Ruine von Kilchurn Castle wieder

landlubbers, the thought of encountering such a giant out there in the inky inlet is a little unsettling. Back into the car. Collecting legends.

The surface of Loch Fyne glistens like a mirror. We follow the road along the northern shoreline and just before Inveraray we reach an old stone bridge that crosses near the mouth of the River Aray. A delightful one-lane traffic light drama – up over the bridge arch, then a great "Oh" and "Ah": As if a giant lawnmower has cut the meadows of the banks, the dark green lawns stretch to the hills beyond, opening a view to Inveraray Castle. The ancestral home of the Duke of Argyll cowers like a medieval spaceship in the landscape, with its sage-green walls and mighty circular towers with steep conical roofs at each corner. The transition between the surrounding wilderness and the carefully manicured castle gardens is barely discernible. Veer right, castle visit. We're plunged into the essence and odiousness of the Campbell clan, a big drama of Scottish history, all myth and dream tanks have been filled up to the brim with such an opportunity.

Leaving Inveraray behind, the A819 follows the river valley of the Aray in sweeping esses. The grippy asphalt and the sun shining down from a clear, blue sky on the riverside meadows simply adds to the sensation: although we have driven pretty much due north to Loch Awe near Cladich, not a single straight stretch can be found on these 15 kilometres. Instead, long, snaking bends lined with birches and seemingly endless green hills flash by. Past the ruins of Kilchurn Castle and on to the east, the scenery now changes. The surrounding hills, carpeted in brown and golden grasses, loom closer. Conifers, planted in well-defined stands, have replaced the leafy thickets of the lower Highland plains in the south. On the A82 to the north of Tyndrum, the landscape becomes virtually treeless, massive mountain peaks tower from the breathtaking scenery of a fantasy film. Millions of years old, the surf-like grass-covered rocks are frozen into gigantic waves.

SKYFALL

nach Osten und nun wandelt sich das Bild: Die umliegenden Hügel rücken näher an die Straße heran, bedeckt von braun und gelb leuchtendem Gras. Nadelbäume, in scharf umrissenen Flicken gepflanzt, haben das Laubdickicht der tieferen Highland-Etagen im Süden abgelöst. Auf der A82 hinter Tyndrum nach Norden ist die Landschaft nahezu baumlos, riesige Bergkegel ragen aus der atemberaubenden Szenerie eines Fantasy-Films. Die Millionen Jahre alte Brandung eines Meeres aus mit Gras bewachsenem Fels ist hier zu Riesenwellen erstarrt, in deren Tal wir uns schüchtern vorwärts bewegen. Alles scheint überdimensioniert, an einem bestimmten Punkt kommen wir uns vor wie Ameisen in den Falten eines Erdoberflächen-Tischtuchs. Bridge of Orchy, vorüber am Loch Tulla, und dann haben wir die Hochebene des Rannoch-Moors rund um Loch Bà erreicht. Pfützen, Tümpel, Teiche sind in das weite Moor-Land eingebettet und bilden ein mit Wasser vollgesogenes Plateau, in dem die großen Wasserflächen des Loch durch schmale Kanäle verbunden sind. Auf Deichen quert die A82 die vollkommen menschenleere Ebene wie ein Fremdkörper, der zurückliegende Sommer hat die spärliche Vegetation in ein dunkles Ockerbraun verfärbt, über dem nun triefende Wolken hängen. Auf dem Weg nach Glencoe türmen sich Bergspitzen, die aus dem Erdinneren hervorgepresst, von vulkanischer Energie geboren und dann vom Eis prähistorischer Gletscher abgeschliffen wurden. Man sieht der archaischen Landschaft, die sich vor uns ausbreitet, ihre gewalttätige Evolution regelrecht an. Schroffe und düstere Berge mit kahlen Schädeln in einer epischen Weite – kein Wunder, dass die Gegend hier oben bereits als Set für die James Bond-Episode „Skyfall" oder die Harry Potter-Filme herhalten musste. Auf einer stählernen Fachwerkbrücke überqueren wir bei Ballachulish den Loch Leven und nehmen dann nach wenigen Meilen bei Corran die kleine Fähre über den Loch Linnhe. Es geht nach Westen ans Meer, bei Glenuig am Atlantik drehen wir bei und driften über Glenfinnan zurück ins Landesinnere. Vorbei an Loch Lochy, in Richtung Norden, die letzten 40 Meilen zur Fähre nach Isle of Skye vergehen wie in Trance. Schottland hat uns mit Haut und Haaren.

Kein Wunder, dass die Gegend hier oben bereits als Set für die James Bond-Episode „Skyfall" oder die Harry Potter-Filme herhalten musste.

It's no wonder that the region up here proved popular as a movie set for James Bond's "Skyfall" or the Harry Potter series.

We drift through the wave troughs in awe. Everything seems gigantic, at times we feel like ants in the folds of earth's tablecloth. The bridge of Orchy, past Loch Tulla, and on to the high plateau of Rannoch Moor around Loch Bà. Puddles, pools and ponds have gathered on the vast moorland to form a waterlogged tableland on which the great expanses of water are connected by narrow channels. The A82 crosses the completely deserted plain like an alien shape on a dyke, the past summer has coloured the sparse vegetation into a dark ochre, over which now dripping clouds hang. On the way to Glencoe the mountain peaks tower, pressed out of the earth's interior, born of volcanic energy and then sanded by the ice of prehistoric glaciers, the archaic landscape reveals to us its violent evolution. Dark and rugged bald-headed mountains in an epic expanse – it's no wonder that the region up here proved popular as a movie set for James Bond's "Skyfall" or the Harry Potter series.

At Ballachulish, we cross Loch Leven on a steel truss bridge and after a few miles catch the small ferry near Corran over Loch Linnhe. We head west to the sea, near Glenuig on the Atlantic we heave-to, then wend back inland after Glenfinnan. Past Loch Lochy, heading north, the last 40 miles to the Isle of Skye ferry pass in a trance. Scotland has captured us body and soul.

HOTELS

OYSTER INN
CONNEL, OBAN PA37 1PJ
TEL. +44 1631 710666
WWW.OYSTERINN.CO.UK

ARDANAISEIG HOTEL
KILCHRENAN, TAYNUILT PA35 1HE
TEL. +44 1866 833333
WWW.ARDANAISEIG.COM

SEAFOOD

LOCHLEVEN SEAFOOD
NICH, FORT WILLIAM PH33 6SA
TEL. +44 1855 821048
WWW.LOCHLEVENSEAFOODCAFE.CO.UK

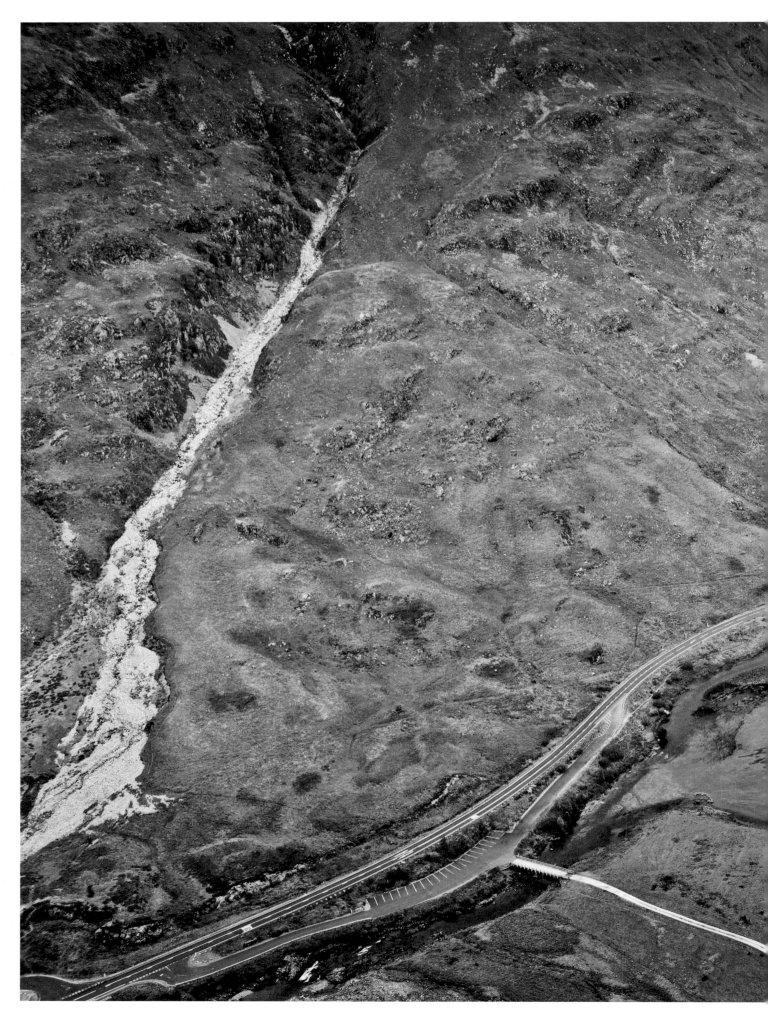

HOTELS

HOTEL EILEAN IARMAIN
SLEAT, ISLE OF SKYE IV43 8QR
TEL. +44 1471 833332
WWW.EILEANIARMAIN.CO.UK

DUISDALE HOUSE HOTEL
ISLEORNSAY, ISLE OF SKYE IV43 8QW
TEL. +44 1471 833202
WWW.DUISDALE.COM

B&B

BRACKEN BRAE B&B
HALF OF 10 CALGARY
ARDVASAR, ISLE OF SKYE IV45 8RU
TEL. +44 1471 844 421
WWW.BRACKENBRAE.COM

GLASGOW ISLE OF SKYE

Glasgow ist kein wirklich beschwingter Einstieg in unsere Schottland-Reise, aber eine Stadt mit Gewicht, die einen gleich in die verwegene, raue Atmosphäre Schottlands zieht. Mit der ersten Tour-Etappe durch den Nationalpark „Loch Lomond and The Trossachs" zeigt sich Schottland noch von seiner eher lieblichen Seite, auch der erste Abstecher ans Meer hat noch weiche Züge für Liebhaber von Natur und Einsamkeit. Spätestens auf der Fahrt übers Rannoch Moor sind wir allerdings im Schottland für Fortgeschrittene angekommen. Die Weite dieser beinahe menschenfeindlichen Landschaft und ihre bedrohliche Schönheit ziehen einen in ihren magischen Bann, touristische Leichtigkeit oder angenehmes Meilenfressen darf hier nicht erwartet werden. Auch auf der Schluss-etappe in Richtung Isle of Skye herrscht die verwunschene Stimmung eines Troll-Thrillers – genau dafür sind wir aber nach Schottland gekommen.

—

Glasgow is not a particularly exciting gateway to our Scotland journey, but it's a city with gravitas, one that pulls you right into the audacious, rugged atmosphere of Scotland. With the first stage of the trip through the national parks of Loch Lomond and The Trossachs, Scotland displays its somewhat gentler side, and the first stretch along the ocean offers softer features for admirers of nature and solitude. But once we reach the Great Moor of Rannoch, we've arrived in Scotland for the advanced. The vastness of this almost hostile landscape and its ominous beauty cast a magical spell, but don't expect an easy Sunday outing or mile upon mile of driving pleasure. And even the final leg towards the Isle of Skye is dominated by the haunted mood of a troll thriller – but that's precisely why we have come to Scotland.

656 KM • 11 STUNDEN // 407 MILES • 11 HOURS

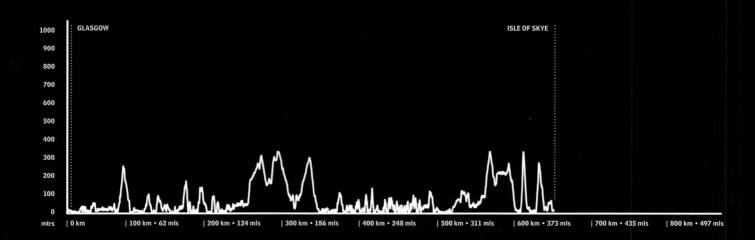

ISLE OF SKYE

220 KM · 4 STUNDEN // 136 MILES · 4 HOURS

Spätestens wenn die kleine Fähre von Glenelg kommend am schmalen Anleger in Kylerhea andockt und die Räder langsam vom stählernen Deck auf die bröckelnde Betonrampe rollen, legt Dein innerer Dudelsack zu einer wahren Pathos-Orgie los: imaginärer Schottland-Soundtrack, eine Kaskade in Gänsehaut. Isle of Skye, wie das schon klingt!

—

When the wee ferry from Glenelg docks at the narrow slipway in Kylerhea and our wheels slowly roll off the steel deck and onto the crumbling concrete ramp, you can bet your inner bagpipes will begin to wail, "Over the Sea to Skye". Isle of Skye – the name alone is enough to raise goosebumps.

Nach blauem, weitem Himmel, nach kreischenden Möwen und die Haare zerzausendem Atlantik-Wind. Dass sich „Skye" eher aus dem gälischen Wort für „Nebel" herleitet, will man da erst einmal überhaupt nicht wissen. Heute scheint über der Kyle Rhea-Meerenge die Sonne, tausende Lichtreflexe tanzen auf den kleinen Wellen, und im Wasser des Sound wabern die dicken, algigen Schlieren des Kelp. Reiseführer-Wetter, der Traum jedes Tourismus-Managers. Die 1600-Quadratkilometer-Insel mit ihren nicht einmal zehntausend Einwohnern ist ein schottischer Mikrokosmos und auf jeden Fall die kurze Fährfahrt wert. Man hätte natürlich auch die Mitte der Neunziger eröffnete Skye Bridge, oben bei Kyle of Lochalsh, nehmen können, aber irgendwie gehört es doch zum Ethos echter Windgesichter, nicht den leichtesten Weg einzuschlagen. Und morgen früh, auf dem Weg zurück in die Highlands, schauen wir uns das moderne Brückending mal an. Man muss es ja nicht übertreiben mit der Romantik.

Heute ist aber Isle of Skye-Time: Slow Food, Slow Drive, Treibenlassen. Eine schmale, einspurige Straße mit gelegentlichen Passagepunkten führt von der Fährstelle weg und zielstrebig bergauf über die Hügel. Bereits nach wenigen Kilometern sehen wir das Meer tief hinter uns. Das langsame Dahinwandern in den Heidekraut- und Farnmatten versetzt einen in vergnügte Trance, Ideallinien und Querkräfte sind uns jetzt völlig egal. Stattdessen wird gelassen dahingezuckelt, bei auftretendem Gegenverkehr überbietet man sich in höflich winkender Hilfsbereitschaft – hier dürfte wohl eher darum gestritten werden, wer als erstes in die nächste Straßenbucht zurücksetzen darf. Dann taucht in der Ferne die Nordküste der Insel auf, aus dem Meer ragt eine Vielzahl von Inseln, unten am Wasser treffen wir auf die A87. Es geht nach links in Richtung Portree, vorbei an den tief eingeschnittenen Buchten des Loch Ainort und des Loch Sligachan. Die umgebenden Hügel trauen sich jetzt kaum bis an die Straße heran, verfolgen uns eine gute halbe Stunde lang mit ihren runden Kuppen und sanften Hängen. Bei Sligachan verlassen wir die A87 deshalb auf der Suche nach Abwechslung in Richtung Carbost. Zwischen

HOTELS

THE THREE CHIMNEYS
COLBOST, DUNVEGAN,
ISLE OF SKYE, IV55 8ZT
TEL. +44 01470 511258
WWW. THREECHIMNEYS.CO.UK

An immense, blue sky, shrieking gulls, hair tussled by a brisk Atlantic breeze. The fact that "Skye" comes from the Gaelic word "fog" is better left forgotten. Today, however, the sun is shining over the Kyle Rhea tidal stream, thousands of lights dance on the ripples of the sounds, thick, leathery strips of kelp billow in the water. Perfect travel weather, the dream of all tourist guides. The 1,600-square-kilometre island with less than ten thousands residents is a Scottish microcosm and definitely worth the short ferry trip. One could, of course, take the Skye Bridge – opened in the mid-nineties – just up from the Kyle of Lochalsh, but somehow it just doesn't fit the ethos of serious weather-beaten roadies to take the easy way. And anyway, tomorrow morning on the way back to the Highlands we'll have a look at the modern bridge. Let's not go overboard with the romantic stuff.

But today it's Isle-of-Skye-time; slow food, slow driving, easy roving. A narrow, one-lane road with occasional passing bays leads away from the ferry landing, steadily climbing up and over the hills. After a few kilometres we see the sea far behind and below us. Our slow tour through the heather and fern carpets lull us into a contented reverie, ideal driving lines and lateral forces are completely irrelevant here. Instead, it's about quietly rambling along, and, if a car should by chance come opposite, rather than trying to squeeze past, each tries to outdo the other in a courteous acquiescence of "please, after you", both eager to be the first to back up to the last passing bay. In the distance, the north coast of the island appears. A cluster of islands poke out of the sea. Down at the coastline we meet up with the A87, turn left, and head to Portree, past the seawater sounds of Loch Ainort and Loch Sligachan. The surrounding hills keep themselves at a distance now, but they shadow us with their rounded brows and gentle slopes for a good half hour. We leave the A87 at Sligachan and head towards Carbost in search of some variety. Spread before us between the mountain peaks are restless pebbles and rubble plains, covered with a thin layer of moss and grass. The now cloudy sky fits this barren landscape perfectly. We've been driving for a good hour now and have barely managed 60 kilometres. Duly sedated, we've only just

Bergkegeln breiten sich unruhige Geröll- und Steinschutt-Ebenen aus, die mit einer dünnen Schicht Moos und Gras bewachsen sind – zu dieser reichlich kargen Landschaft passt der nun wieder trübe Himmel ausgezeichnet. Wir sind mittlerweile eine gute Stunde unterwegs, haben kaum 60 Kilometer geschafft und landen reichlich sediert auf der Westseite der Isle. Große Naturwunder sind bis jetzt ausgeblieben, die Straße ist ein langer, ruhiger Fluss – wir schalten also auf Plan B, um etwas Würze in den Tag zu kippen: In Carbost, einer Ansammlung von niedrigen, weißen Häusern am Ufer des Loch Harport, sitzt seit 1831 Talisker, die einzige Single Malt-Whiskybrennerei der ganzen Insel Skye. Blockige Hallen mit weißen Fassaden und kleinen Fenstern, ein Münzwurf entscheidet, wer im Besucherzentrum bis zur Whiskyprobe bleiben und wer sich dann eben nur schwelgerische Geschichten von würzigem Temperament, Rauch und Torf, Chili-Noten und frischen Zitronengras-Ahnungen anhören darf.

Eine spannende Stunde und wenige Whisky-Zungenküsse später steht fest, dass Whiskyproben nicht zwingend im Fankurven-Delirium weißweinseliger Mosel-Abenteuer enden müssen: Wir rollen ohne Fahne, ohne schwere Synapsen und im Vollbesitz unserer mentalen Kräfte vom Parkplatz der Brennerei, im Kofferraum sind vier Flaschen „Talisker 10 Jahre" sicher verstaut – an die weit über 350 Pfund teure Flasche „Talisker 30 Jahre" hat sich dann doch niemand getraut. Wir treten den Rückzug auf der bekannten Straße nach Sligachan an, zielen dann nach Norden und stellen bei Portree erfreut fest, dass sich auf unseren Zungen erst jetzt auch der letzte Rest von Torfaroma verflüchtigt hat. Was nicht weiter tragisch ist, zumal sich jetzt die kleine Straße über Drumuie zum Loch Snizort Beag aus Leibeskräften um gute Unterhaltung und lang anhaltendes Aroma bemüht: fröhliches Dahinschnüren auf einem winzigen Asphaltband, immer weiter bis Uig. Hier endet die A87 im Fähranleger zur Isle of Harris, gleich hinter der Bucht schwingt sich die vorher abzweigende A855 aber in zwei deftigen Rampen samt einer kernigen 90-Grad-Kehre den Berg hinauf. Kurz vor Erreichen der nächsten Höhenlage über Uig erwischen wir gerade noch den Rechts-Abzweig Rich-

Heute ist aber Isle of Skye-Time: Slow Food, Slow Drive, Treibenlassen. Eine schmale, einspurige Straße mit gelegentlichen Passagepunkten führt von der Fährstelle weg und zielstrebig bergauf über die Hügel.

But today it's Isle-of-Skye-time; slow food, slow driving, easy roving. A narrow, one-lane road with occasional passing bays leads away from the ferry landing, steadily climbing up and over the hills.

arrived on the west coast of the isle. Until now, great miracles of nature have evaded us. The road is a long, smooth asphalt river – to add a little spice to the day we switch to plan B: In Carbost, a cluster of low, white houses on the shore of Loch Harport has been home to Talisker since 1831, the only single malt scotch whisky distillery on the whole Isle of Skye. Solid angular buildings with white facades and small windows, the flip of a coin decides who will take part in the whisky tasting and who will be sentenced to just listen to the rich stories of spicy tendencies, smoke and peat, notes of chilli and hints of fresh lemongrass.

After a fascinating hour with a few whisky revelations on the tongue, we've discovered that whisky tastings don't necessarily have to end in the same way as the staggering delirium of a white wine adventure on the Mosel: We roll from the parking area of the distillery without reeking of scotch, with fully-functioning synapses and in full possession of our faculties, as well as four bottles of 10-year-old Talisker safely stowed in the boot – nobody was courageous enough to buy Talisker's £350 bottle of 30-year-old single malt. We backtrack to the familiar road to Sligachan before heading north and happily discover in Portree that only now the last vestiges of peat aroma have evaporated from our tongues. This is not a tragedy, especially since the little road via Drumuie to Loch Snizort Beag endeavours with might and main to provide good entertainment and long-lasting aromas: Happy meandering on the tiny strip of asphalt on and on

tung An Taobh Sear – und nun beginnt ganz großes Kino: Sanft schwingend fließt ein Asphaltband, das kaum Auto-Breite besitzt, nach Nordosten, und plötzlich öffnet sich eine Hochebene zu sprachlos machender Dramatik. Dann taucht in der Ferne ein letzter, mächtiger Bergrücken auf. Die schmale Straße zielt direkt darauf zu, schmiegt sich zwischen die Hügel des Hochmoors, steigt aber die ganze Zeit immer höher hinauf. Nach wenigen Kilometern scheint die ganze Landschaft keine Lust mehr auf Verspieltheit zu haben, alles spannt sich hin zu dem massigen Berg, der nun an seinem rechten Abriss gewaltige Felszähne bleckt. Mit ein paar letzten nachlässig hingeworfenen Kurven erreicht die Straße den höchsten Punkt, links und rechts steht schwarzes Wasser in kleinen Pfützen zwischen Gras und Moos, dann brüllt uns eine ganze Batterie von zerschossenen Verkehrsschildern letzte Warnungen zu: Gefälle, Kehren, Steinschlag. Wir werfen das Auto in eine scharfe Rechtskehre und finden uns in der Südostflanke des Quiraing wieder. Dass sich diese Abfahrt ein wenig anfühlt wie der wilde Ritt auf dem Hosenboden, kommt nicht von ungefähr: So weit das Auge reicht – und es reicht weit, bis zum viele Kilometer entfernten Meer – besteht die Landschaft aus Felsabstürzen und Erdrutschen. Schlecht kaschierte Baustellen und Asphaltflicken machen klar, dass sich die Quiraing-Passstraße immer noch, immer wieder auf Talfahrt befindet. In so einer Situation wird Straßenbau zur temporären, flexiblen Angelegenheit.

Kaum vorzustellen, auf dieser Straße im Winter oder bei dichtem Nebel unterwegs zu sein. Als wir bei Staffin die Küstenebene erreichen, flattern uns selbst an diesem milden Herbsttag die Hände. Am Besten: Umdrehen! Und nochmal! Die wiedergefundene A855 in Richtung Süden hat aber auch ein paar Überraschungen parat. Am Kilt Rock Viewpoint stellen wir fest, dass das zu unserer Linken liegende Meer gute 50 Meter unter der Küstenlinie liegt. Ein kleiner Was-

to Uig. Here the A87 ends at the ferry landing to the Isle of Harris. But just past the bay, the A855 climbs up the mountainside in two steep stretches connected by a sharp 90-degree corner. Shortly before reaching the next elevation over Uig we discover, in the nick of time, a turnoff to the right towards An Taobh Sear and here the blockbuster begins: snaking in gentle sweeps to the northeast is an asphalt strip that is barely the width of a vehicle, suddenly opening up to a high plateau with a scene that takes your breath away. In the distance a last mighty mountain ridge appears. The narrow road aims directly at it, burrowed between the hills of the high moors, but all the time rising higher and higher. After several kilometres it seems that the whole landscape has no desire to play anymore, everything stretches up to the massive mountain on which mighty rocks snarl on the right escarpment. After the last few carelessly flung corners, the road reaches the highest point. To the left and right black water tarns pool between grass and moss, then an entire battery of bullet-ridden traffic signs screams a final warning: steep grades, hairpins, rockfall – we throw the car into a sharp right-hander and find ourselves back on the southeast flank of Quiraing. It's no coincidence that this downhill spin feels a bit like riding by the seat of your pants: As far as the eye can see, and it can see over many kilometres all the way to the ocean, the landscape is scarred with rock and landslides. Forgotten roadwork sites and surface repairs make it obvious that the Quiraing pass road has been and still is on the slippery downhill slope and, in such situations, road construction can only be a temporary, flexible matter.

It is hard to imagine being on this road in winter or in thick fog. When we reach the coastal plain at Staffin, our hands are shaking, even on this mild autumn day. The best thing would be to turn around and do it all again! Back on the A855 heading to the south, however, a few surprises still await

serfall gischtet über die Kante der senkrecht abfallenden Basalt-Türme ins tief unten auf Felsbrocken brandende Meer. Einige Meilen weiter wandelt sich die Szenerie zu beinahe alpinen Dimensionen: Am Ende der steil vom Meer aus ansteigenden Hänge türmen sich die Felsformationen des Old Man of Storr – Miniatur-Dolomiten mit Ozeanblick hoch oben im Norden.

Zurück in Portree haben wir die spektakuläre Runde über den Norden der Isle of Skye abgeschlossen und machen uns auf den langen Weg zur Brücke. Kyle of Lochalsh, Handbremswende auf den Parkplatz eines Seafood-Restaurants und dann schwärmen. Oder schweigen.

us. At Kilt Rock viewpoint we discover that the sea to the left is a good 50 metres below the coastline, a small waterfall spills over the edge of the vertical basalt towers, falling sharply into the waves crashing on the rocks below. Several miles further on the scenery transforms into almost alpine dimensions. At the end of the steep slopes rising from the sea are the rock formations of the Old Man of Storr – miniature Dolomites but with an ocean view in the far north. Back in Portree we've completed the spectacular loop over the north of the Isle of Skye and start our long way back to the bridge. Kyle of Lochalsh, handbrake turn into the parking area of a seafood restaurant...to bliss. Or silence.

OLD MAN OF STORR

ISLE OF SKYE

Anfahrt über die kleine Fähre von Glenelg nach Kylerhea, dann nach Norden: Wer die rund 200 Kilometer lange Etappe über die Isle of Skye nonstop durchfährt, dürfte dafür rund vier Stunden brauchen – allerdings ist das hier kaum zu erwarten. Im Wesentlichen verläuft die Route über schmale Single Track Roads, auf denen höchste Vorsicht und moderates Tempo angesagt sind. Nicht selten tauchen entgegenkommende Fahrzeuge erst im letzten Moment hinter einem Fels-brocken oder aus kaum wahrnehmbaren Bodensenken auf, hinzu kommen halbwilde Schafe, die plötzlich mitten auf der Fahrbahn stehen. Abgesehen von diesen Sicherheitshinweisen bremst die Isle of Skye aber vor allem durch ihre Schönheit: Von lieblich bis schroff verführt eine sagenhafte Landschaft mit eigentümlich ruhiger Atmosphäre zum Anhalten und Umsehen. Erst die wilde, abenteuerliche und umwerfend dramatische Passstraße am Quiraing lässt einen in hechelnden CURVES-Modus verfallen. Am Ende des Tages hat man sich dann auch die bequeme Fahrt aufs Festland über die Brücke bei Kyle of Lochalsh mehr als verdient.

—

Take the small ferry from Glenelg to Kylerhea, then head north. The entire 200 kilometres around the Isle of Skye in one go take about four hours – but this is unrealistic. Essentially, the route runs over narrow one-lane roads which require utmost caution and moderate speeds. Not infrequently, oncom-ing vehicles appear suddenly from behind a boulder or from barely perceptible hollows, added to this are the semi-wild sheep that often like to stand in the middle of the road. Apart from these cautionary tips, the excursion around the Isle of Skye is slow thanks to its beauty: from charming to rugged, this stunning landscape seduces travellers to linger and soak in its strangely tranquil atmosphere. Finally, in true CURVES manner, the wild, adventurous and breathtakingly dramatic pass road at Quiraing leaves us panting breathlessly. At the end of the day, the pleasant drive to the mainland over the bridge at Kyle of Lochalsh is well-earned.

220 KM • 4 STUNDEN // 136 MILES • 4 HOURS

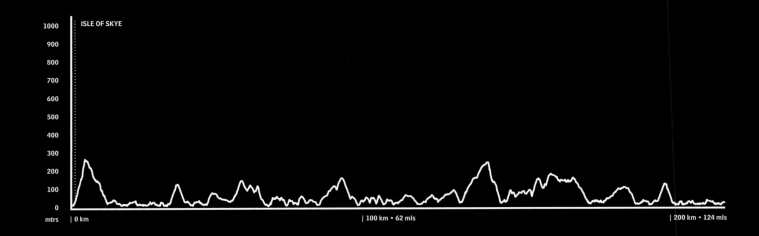

ISLE OF SKYE
ULLAPOOL

280 KM · 5 STUNDEN // 174 MILES · 5 HOURS

So viel Zeit muss sein: Was wir gestern auf der Fähre zur Isle of Skye noch über Warmduscher, Weicheier und Brückenbenutzer gelästert haben, bereuen wir von ganzem Herzen. Die harmonisch zu einem kühnen Buckel geschwungene Brücke zwischen Skye und Kyle of Lochalsh gehört auf alle Fälle zu den Exemplaren, die auch einen emotionalen Sinn erfüllen und nicht nur rationale Verkehrsbeschleunigung zum Ziel haben.

—

Do yourself a favour: We now very much regret the way we griped about the wimps, sissies and bridge-users on our ferry trip to the Isle of Skye yesterday. The bridge between Skye and Kyle of Lochalsh, which harmoniously arcs to a bold bow, definitely belongs to the specimens that also strike an emotional balance and are not purely aiming for a functional flow of traffic.

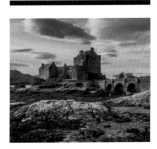

INVERARAY CASTLE

EILEAN DONAN CASTLE
DORNIE, KYLE OF LOCHALSH IV40 8DX
WWW.EILEANDONANCASTLE.COM

Als Gesamtinszenierung zwischen den Bergen rundum und über das im Wasser des Fjord spiegelnde Himmelblau sowie ein paar vorgelagerte Inselchen hüpfend macht die kaum zwei Minuten währende Überfahrt große Freude. Rechts grüßt die Ruine der Caisteal Maol, einer alten Wikingerburg, von der aus in grauer Vorzeit durch eine im Wasser gespannte Kette vorbeifahrende Schiffe ausgebremst und dann zur Kasse gebeten wurden. Glücklicherweise haben sich die modernen Nachfahren der Nordmänner hieran kein Beispiel genommen; die Brückenpassage aufs Festland oder in umgekehrter Richtung nach Skye ist völlig kostenfrei. Von wegen „Früher war alles besser".

Bei Auchtertyre müssten wir uns eigentlich der nach Norden führenden A890 anvertrauen, nur wenige Meilen weiter östlich wartet aber Eilean Donan Castle auf einen Besuch. Man hat den Namen eventuell noch nicht gehört und tut sich mit der gälischen Aussprache guttural gurgelnd reichlich schwer, aber es gibt keinen Schottland-Kalender ohne dramatisches Eilean Donan-Motiv. Filmliebhaber dürften die Burg übrigens auch als Sitz des schottischen MI6-Hauptquartiers kennen – unvergessen ist die Szene aus „The World Is Not Enough", in der Geheimdienst-Tüftler Q James Bond die Verwendung von Dudelsäcken als Maschinengewehr demonstriert. Die Ansicht der Burg auf einer kleinen Insel direkt am Ufer des Loch Duich mit der steinernen Brücke und den Bergen der Isle of Skye im Hintergrund wirkt aber auch beinahe inszeniert-kitschig: Hier schalten ganze Reisebusladungen von Schottland-Touristen ihre Fotokameras auf Dauerklick, und dass nicht alle paar Minuten jemand beim „Selfie mit #burginschottland #hammer" rückwärts in den Loch fällt, grenzt an ein Wunder. Dabei ist Eilean Donan nicht nur ein ikono-

It's an all-embracing work of art of the surrounding mountains, of the blue sky mirrored in the water of the loch, with several islets adding to the great delight of this less than two-minute crossing. To the right stand the ruins of Caisteal Maol, an old Viking fortress, the inhabitants of which spanned a heavy chain across the straight to stop ships and levy a toll. Luckily, the modern descendants of the Northerners did not use this as an example. The crossing is now toll-free in both directions. Who says everything was better in the olden days.

At Auchtertyre we should continue north on the A890, but after just a few miles the Eilean Donan Castle to the east calls us. The name may not be familiar, and the guttural-gurgling Gaelic pronunciation doesn't help, but no Scottish calendar is complete without a month dedicated to the dramatic Eilean Donan. Film buffs may also recognise the castle as the Scottish MI6 headquarters. In the one unforgettable scene from "The World Is Not Enough", the secret service gadget guru "Q" demonstrates to James Bond how to use a machine gun disguised as bagpipes. The view of the castle on the tiny isle directly on the banks of Loch Duich with the stone bridge and the mountains of Skye in the background seems like orchestrated kitsch. Here, busloads of tourists take bursts of photos and every few minutes someone snaps a selfie with #castleinscotland #awesome. It's a miracle that no one falls backwards into the loch. But Eilean Donan is not just a pretty picture, it's also the point of crystallisation of Scotland's past: Here, Picts cudgelled the Gaels, Scots battered the Vikings, here the Mackenzie and MacDonald clans clashed for centuries in bloody feuds, here the Jacobite rebels and Spanish soldiers gathered in anticipation of a Highland insurrection against the English crown. In April 1719, the Royal Navy sent frigates to the area,

Hier schalten ganze Reisebusladungen von Schottland-Touristen ihre Fotokameras auf Dauerklick, und dass nicht alle paar Minuten jemand beim „Selfie mit #burginschottland #hammer" rückwärts in den Loch fällt, grenzt an ein Wunder.

Here, busloads of tourists take bursts of photos and every few minutes someone snaps a selfie with #castleinscotland #awesome. It's a miracle that no one falls backwards into the loch.

grafisches Fotomotiv, sondern auch ein Kristallisationspunkt schottischer Geschichte: Hier prügelten sich Pikten und Scoten, schlugen sich Schotten und Wikinger, hier trugen die Clans der Mackenzies und MacDonalds in verbissener Eintracht über Jahrhunderte hinweg blutige Rivalitäten aus, hier versammelten sich jakobitische Rebellen und spanische Soldaten in Erwartung eines Highlander-Aufstands gegen die englische Krone. Mit dem Resultat, dass Eilean Donan Castle im April 1719 von Fregatten der Royal Navy unter Beschuss genommen, erobert und dann in die Luft gesprengt wurde. Es folgte eine äußerst friedliche Sendepause am Loch für über 200 Jahre, und erst 1920 ging es mit Rekonstruktionsarbeiten weiter, an deren Ende die heutige museale Verwendung stand. Irgendwie auch gut so.

Nach einem Rundgang durch die Burg haben wir aber auch schon die Nase voll von geführter Touristik. Spätestens, als wir die schlüpfrigen Zoten zweier deutscher Touristen über den benachbarten „Loch Long" in kalkulierter Hörweite ihrer recht ansehnlichen Reiseleiterin mit anhören müssen (nur als Verständnis-Tipp: Englischsprachigen Lesern könnte etwas ähnliches am bayrischen Berg „Wank" oder am „Titisee" im Schwarzwald passieren), ist uns klar, dass es Zeit für eine einsame Tour nach Norden ist. Zurück auf die A890 bei Auchtertyre, dann bis Strathcarron und eine gute Meile später nach links auf die A896 in Richtung Lochcarron abbiegen. 15 Kilometer später ist am Bealach Café die Abzweigung zum Applecross-Pass erreicht. Bereits die farbigen Warnschilder stellen unseren inneren Colin McRae scharf: Die Straße sei bei Winterwet-

bombarded then conquered Eilean Donan Castle, and then blew up what remained. For the next 200 years things stayed relatively quiet at the loch, and it was only in 1920 that reconstruction continued, ending in the wonderful museum that stands there today. Somehow good in a way. After a look around the castle we've had enough of guided tours. Having to listen to the suggestive comments about the neighbouring Loch Long from two German tourists within earshot of their rather attractive tour guide (English-speaking readers might make similar comments about the Bavarian mountain "Wank" or "Titisee" in the Black Forest), we realise it's time for us to continue our solitary tour north.

Back on the A890 at Auchtertyre, on to Strathcarron and a good mile later we turn left onto the A896 towards Lochcarron. After about 15 kilometres at the Bealach Café we reach the turnoff to Applecross Pass. The colourful warning signs awaken our inner Colin McRae, the roads in winter are "normally impassable", we're cautioned about high altitudes, steep gradients and tight corners. In fact, the "Bealach na Bà" or the Applecross Pass, is "not advised for learner drivers, very large vehicles or caravans". Perfect!

For the first mile or so, learner drivers, large vehicles and campers are spared, but then things turn hairy: it's only eight tight kilometres from sea level to the top of the mountain saddle at 600 metres, and the panoramic view over Loch Kishorn is indescribable. The sun glistens on the water, the Allt a'Chumhaing River winds its way through the wide valley, the surrounding mountains blush in the rusty hues of ferns, mosses and dry

RESTAURANT
APPLECROSS INN
SHORE ST, APPLECROSS,
STRATHCARRON IV54 8LR
TEL: +44 1520 744262
WWW.APPLECROSS.UK.COM/INN/

HOTELS

SHIELDAIG LODGE
BADACHRO, GAIRLOCH, ROSS-SHIRE
IV21 2AN
TEL: +44 1445 741333
WWW.SHIELDAIGLODGE.COM

....

THE TORRIDON
ACHNASHEEN,
WESTER ROSS IV22 2EY
TEL: +44 1445 700300
WWW.THETORRIDON.COM

....

POOL HOUSE
POOLEWE ACHNASHEEN,
WESTER ROSS IV22 2LD
TEL: +44 1445 781272
WWW.POOL-HOUSE.CO.UK

....

SUMMER ISLES
ADRESSE: ACHILTIBUIE, ULLAPOOL
IV26 2YG
TEL: +44 1854 622282
WWW.SUMMERISLESHOTEL.COM

ter „normally impassable", es wird vor großer Höhe gewarnt, vor heftigen Steigungen und scharfen Kehren und ganz allgemein sei der „Bealach na Bà", der Applecross-Pass, „not advised for learner drivers, large vehicles and campers". Herrlich!

Eine gute Meile weit werden Fahranfänger, große Fahrzeuge und Wohnmobile noch geschont, dann geht es zur Sache: Von Meereshöhe geht es auf nur acht Kilometern stramme 600 Höhenmeter in den Bergsattel empor, der Panoramablick über Loch Kishorn ist unbeschreiblich. Die Sonne glitzert auf der Wasseroberfläche, der Flusslauf des Allt a' Chumhaing windet sich durchs weit ausgebreitet daliegende Tal, die Berge ringsum leuchten im tiefen Orangeton von trockenem Farn, Moos und verdörrtem Gras. Das Auto turnt die steilen Rampen hinauf, wirbelt um Serpentinen und Kehren, fliegt regelrecht auf einem beklemmend schmalen Asphaltband durch den mächtigen Kessel bis zur Passhöhe. Zumindest – fast: Natürlich presst sich am Ende doch ein „Learner Driver im Camper" den Berg hinauf, aber wir sind von dieser majestätischen Landschaft so hingerissen, dass wir den im Schritttempo dahinzuckelnden weißen Plastikriesen als Safety Car sehen und geduldig in seinem Schlepptau bis zum Aussichtspunkt rollen. Erwartungsgemäß legen Maud und Brian aus Brighton hier eine verschwitzte Pause ein, werfen den Campingbrenner an, um sich einen Tee zu kochen und fragen sich dann staunend, wie sie wohl jemals wieder hier herunter kommen. Unsere Chance für ein freundlich winkendes, betont gönnerhaftes Überholmanöver – und es reicht sogar noch für ein andächtiges Erinnerungsfoto rüber zur Isle of Skye: #hammer #selfiemitautoundkumpel #bestestrassederwelt.

grasses. The car weaves its way up the steep single-track road, sweeping through twists and turns, almost flying over the nightmarishly narrow asphalt strip and through the mighty cauldron up to the pass. Well, almost. Of course, we encounter a "learner driver in a camper van" crawling up the mountainside, but we're so blown away by the majestic landscape that we're happy to patiently doddle along at walking speed behind the white plastic giant safety car to the viewpoint. As expected, Maud and Brian from Brighton take a sweaty break here, they fire up the camp cooker for a cuppa and are probably wondering how they're supposed to get down again. This is our chance for a friendly wave and a wide swerve around them –we even have time for an obligatory souvenir photo over to the Isle of Skye: #awesome #selfiewithcarandmate #bestroadintheworld.

We think our camping friends will probably find the quiet, considerably more gradual downhill drive to the west and Applecross Bay much less stressful than the brutal climb from the east. When we return over the pass after our seafood stop in Applecross there is no sign of a caravan anywhere, hence we assume that the happy campers, out of concern for their brakes, have opted to return to Loch Carron via the ring road around the Applecross peninsula. And we're right... almost: Shortly before Tornapress we encounter Mr Campervan, but he's now on a racing bike, having just careened through the corners of Bealach na Bà, and is now pedalling north at an impressive tempo. He's hoping to rendezvous with the lady of his heart, who has indeed taken the alternative, twisting Applecross northern loop, at Shieldaig. She'll cycle the next spectacular leg, because she's fitter, after all, and hence he

Die ruhige, deutlich flachere Abfahrt nach Westen zur Applecross Bay dürfte unsere Camping-Freunde vermutlich weniger stressen als der brutale Anstieg aus östlicher Richtung, befinden wir. Als nach unserem Seafood-Stopp in Applecross auf dem Rückweg über den Pass tatsächlich weit und breit kein Camper zu sehen ist, vermuten wir sogar, dass die Wohnmobilisten für ihren Rückweg zum Loch Carron aus Sorge um die Bremsen ihres Campers lieber die Ringstraße um die Applecross-Halbinsel herum genommen haben. Und wir liegen – wenigstens zur Hälfte – richtig: Kurz vor Tornapress treffen wir den Herrn des Camper-Duos, der sich völlig sorglos auf einem Rennrad die Kehren des Bealach na Bà hinuntergestürzt hat und nun mit beachtlichem Reisetempo in Richtung Norden unterwegs ist. Er hoffe, die tatsächlich über den Applecross-Nord-Loop kurvende Dame seines Herzens bei Shieldaig wiederzutreffen, erklärt er. Die nächste tolle Strecke sei dann ihr Fahrrad-Turn und da sie fitter wäre, blieben ihm eh nur die Abfahrten (verschmitztes Grinsen aus rot tränenden Augen) ... Wir tun insgeheim stille Buße über unsere Vorurteile und wünschen dem vitalen Duo viel Spaß.

Wir folgen weiter dem schottischen Beitrag zu den Traumstraßen der Welt. Die große „NC500"-Runde von Inverness einmal um den Norden Schottlands herum hat ihren Namen aufgrund einer Streckenführung von rund 500 Meilen Länge – bis zu unserem Etappenziel bei Ullapool haben wir nun noch einmal 90 Meilen von 500 vor uns. Und die internationalen Vergleiche mit kalifornischem Pacific Coast Highway oder südafrikanischer Garden Route sind keineswegs an den Haaren herbeigezogen: Die Landschaften zwischen dem 1010 Meter hohen Benn Eighe-Massiv, Loch Maree, Loch Ewe und dem Little Loch Broom sind begeisternd schön. Interessanteste Feststellung kurz vor Ullapool: Man kann sich an so viel Panorama, Majestät und Drama einfach nicht gewöhnen.

Wir folgen weiter dem schottischen Beitrag zu den Traumstraßen der Welt. Die große „NC500"-Runde von Inverness einmal um den Norden Schottlands herum hat ihren Namen aufgrund einer Streckenführung von rund 500 Meilen Länge.

We continue along Scotland's equivalent of the world's dream roads, the great "NC500" loop from Inverness up and around the northern tip of Scotland got its name from its length of 500 miles.

tackles "just the downhill bits." A mischievous grin and bloodshot, streaming eyes... Secretly we retract our preconceptions and wish the dynamic couple a lot of fun.

We continue along Scotland's equivalent of the world's dream roads, the great "NC500" loop from Inverness up and around the northern tip of Scotland got its name from its length of 500 miles – from here to the destination of our leg in Ullapool we still have 90 of those 500 ahead of us.

Comparing this stretch to California's Pacific Coast Highway or South Africa's Garden Route is not at all far-fetched. The landscapes between the 1,010-metre Beinn Eighe massif, Loch Maree, Loch Ewe and Little Loch Broom are inspiringly beautiful. An interesting observation just before Ullapool: You can simply never tire of such panorama, majesty and magnificence.

ISLE OF SKYE ULLAPOOL

Mit einem Besuch des Eilean Donan Castle starten wir historisch und touristisch hochwertig in die dritte Tagesetappe, danach geht es weiter in nördlicher Richtung zur Applecross-Halbinsel. Der sogenannte Bealach na Bà, also „Vieh-Pass", wurde nach den Viehtreibern früherer Jahrhunderte benannt, war einmal der einzige Weg zur Westseite der Insel und ist noch immer ein fahrerisches Sahnestück. Wer nicht über den Pass und wieder zurück fahren möchte, kann heutzutage eine Rundfahrt um die gesamte Halbinsel unternehmen: von Lochcarron kommend über den Pass nach Applecross, weiter zum Loch Shieldaig und am Torridon-Massiv wieder zurück nach Süden. Es empfiehlt sich jedoch eine Fahrt im Uhrzeigersinn, da das extreme Gefälle am Bealach na Bà harmonischer als Bergauf-Passage genommen wird. Wir folgen nach unserer Tour über die Halbinsel dem Verlauf der Westküste bis nach Ullapool und schließen dort die dritte Etappe ab.

—

We start the tour of day three with a worthwhile historic and touristy visit to Eilean Donan Castle before heading north towards the Applecross peninsula. The so-called Bealach na Bà, or pass of the cattle, was historically used as a drover's road, it was the only route to the west side of the island and is a motorist's paradise. Nowadays, those who would prefer not to make the return trip over the pass can take the route around the entire peninsula: From Lochcarron over the pass to Applecross, on to Loch Shieldaig and at the Torridon massif back to the south. The recommendation is to drive in a clockwise direction, since the extreme downhill gradient at Bealach na Bà is more harmonious than the uphill passage. After our tour around the peninsula, we continue along the west coast to Ullapool and that concludes the third leg.

280 KM • 5 STUNDEN // 174 MILES • 5 HOURS

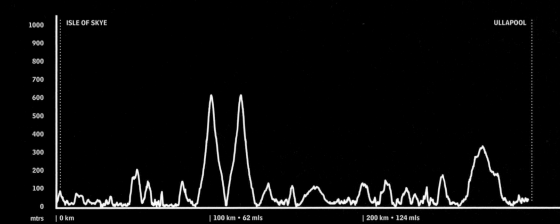

ULLAPOOL INVERNESS

310 KM · CA. 5 STUNDEN // 193 MILES · 5 HOURS

Was für ein Tag. Zwischen kulinarischen Tiefpunkten und emotionalen Gipfeln schlingernd, erspart uns Schottland im hohen Norden heute überhaupt nichts. Los geht es bereits beim Frühstück: Unsere übliche frühmorgendliche Koffein-Injektion direkt in die Herz-Vorkammern, ohne die normalerweise nichts läuft, haben wir schon seit Tagen auf Breakfast Tea umgestellt.

—

What a day. Seesawing between the culinary lowlights and emotional highlights, the far north of Scotland doesn't hold back. It already starts at breakfast: In the last few days we've switched from our usual and highly necessary early morning coffee fix directly into the artery to breakfast tea.

HOTELS

BUNCHREW HOUSE
INVERNESS IV3 8TA
TEL: +44 1463 234917
WWW.BUNCHREWHOUSEHOTEL.COM

....

BOATH HOUSE
BOATH HOUSE, AULDEARN,
NAIRN IV12 5TE
TEL: 44 1667 454896
WWW.BOATH-HOUSE.COM

....

„Scottish Breakfast Tea", wohlgemerkt, das zumindest verkündet der am Kännchen baumelnde Papieranhänger mit patriotischem Stolz. Die englische Variante scheint es nicht über den Hadrianswall zu schaffen. Wir sind zu Tee-Junkies geworden, eine kleine Reise-Thermoskanne im Cupholder transportiert mild gesüßten Schwarztee mit einem Schuss Sahne auch unterwegs und wird bei Foto- und Staune-Stopps genießerisch herumgereicht. Hände wohlig um die heiße Blechtasse gelegt immer wieder genüsslich schlürfen, dabei auf einem Felsbrocken im Wind stehen und auf ein karges Moor hinausblicken oder auf das weite Meer und vorgelagerte Inseln: Ah, Schottland!

Langsam haben wir uns auch an Bohnen zum Frühstück gewöhnt. An labbriges Weißbrot, das vor einem Meeting mit bitterer Orangenmarmelade eine Runde übers Förderband des Toasters drehen muss. An fleischige Speckscheiben und sogar an den obligatorischen Black Pudding. Angelsachsen mögen sich über unser anfängliches Zögern am Frühstücksbuffet wundern, aber für Festlandeuropäer ist die Vorstellung, beim Frühstück dunkelbraune, fast schwarze Blutwurstscheiben in sich hineinzuschaufeln, tatsächlich mehr als skurril. Und dann klebt da plötzlich dieses dunkle Krümelzeug in einer Schale unter der Lampe des Heizstrahlers, um das sich selbst die Locals ehrfurchtsvoll drücken. „Haggis", flüstert uns eine adrett frisierte Mittsechzigerin zu, gefolgt von einem bedeutungsvollen Blick, der alles zwischen „Haben Sie gehört, Schottland hat England den Krieg erklärt" bis „Heute Nacht ist am Strand von Loch Ness der tote Körper eines 15 Meter langen Plesiosauriers angeschwemmt worden" bedeuten kann. Haggis also. Hat man schon einmal gehört, vermutlich in einer Unterhaltung über die ekligsten Speisen der Welt, über Kakerlaken im Salat, verfaulte isländische Hai-Steaks, sardischen Fliegenlarvenkäse, fermentierte Eier oder Rocky

And not just any old brew but "Scottish Breakfast Tea", as the paper tag dangling from the teapot announces with patriotic pride. The English variety seems not to have managed the vault over Hadrian's Wall. We've turned into avid tea-drinkers, and on our photo-and-marvel stops we now have a wee travel thermos in the cupholder filled with slightly sweetened black tea and topped with a dollop of cream. Hands blissfully wrapped around the hot metal cup, taking slurps of the steaming brew while standing on a boulder in the wind and looking out over peaty moors to the island-dotted sea. Ah, Scotland!

We've also become accustomed to eating beans for breakfast. And soft, doughy white bread that has gone once around the conveyor belt of the toaster before being smothered with bitter orange marmalade. And fleshy bacon strips and the obligatory black pudding. Anglo-Saxons may wonder at our initial hesitation at the breakfast buffet, but for Continental Europeans the idea of eating black blood sausage for breakfast is really rather bizarre. But wait. What's that dark crumbly stuff in a bowl under the heat lamps of the buffet that even the locals reverently bypass. "Haggis" whispers a sprucely-coiffed lady in her mid-sixties, at the same time giving us a meaningful look which could possibly mean anything between "have you heard that Scotland has declared war on England" to "last night the dead body of a 15-metre Plesiosaurus washed up on the shores of Loch Ness." Haggis. Perhaps you've heard of it. Probably in a conversation about the world's most disgusting foods, about cockroaches in salads, rotten Icelandic shark steaks, putrid Sardinian fly larvae cheese, fermented eggs or mountain oysters. "Isn't this sheep's innards stuffed in a sheep's stomach?" someone squeals with a trembling voice. While everyone gathers around at a safe distance to stare at the display, a broad-shouldered Scotsman with a ruddy glow to his face

Weshalb bauen Menschen hier, in einer baumlosen Endlosigkeit, am gefühlten Ende der Welt, eine Burg und ein Herrenhaus? Schutz gegen wen? Herr über was? Die alte, jahrhundertelange Abgeschlossenheit Schottlands scheint für ein paar Augenblicke, während wir zaghaft um die Ruinen trotten, Gestalt zu gewinnen.

Why would people build a castle here in this treeless endlessness at what feels like the end of the world? Protection against whom? Lord over what? For a few moments, the old, century-long insularity of Scotland is palpable as we scamper tentatively around the ruins.

Mountain-Austern. „Ist das nicht Schafsdarm mit Schafsdarm-Füllung?", röchelt jemand mit zitternder Stimme, während sich alle in gebührendem Sicherheitsabstand um die Auslage scharen. Zumindest so lange, bis sich ein breitschultriger Schotte mit äußerst gesunder Gesichtsfarbe ellbogenschubsend durch die Menge drängt, um eine ordentliche Portion des dunkelbraunen Krümelbreis feixend auf seinen Teller zu schaufeln. „Na prima," grinst ein Beobachter, „der isst jetzt den Teller nicht leer und wir haben den Salat, weil die Sonne nicht scheint ..."

Gemessen am fast spätsommerlichen Wetter mit blauem Himmel und Schäfchenwolken auf den ersten 30 Meilen von Ullapool bis Unapool scheint unser schottischer Freund aber die Platte tatsächlich gründlich leergeputzt zu haben. Die Fahrt auf der „North 500-Route" über das Fischerdörfchen Ardmair, Knockan Craig bis zum Loch Assynt entfaltet eine besondere Magie: Die Sonne streichelt das trockene Gras der Täler beinahe zärtlich, die klare Luft des Nordens lässt das Licht fast glasig wirken. In der Ferne heben sich die einsamen Bergspitzen des Cul Mor und des Canisp empor, und diese menschenleere Anderweltigkeit findet ihren Höhepunkt an den Ruinen von Ardvreck Castle: Am Ufer des Loch Assynt ragt die bedrohliche Ardvreck-Ruine auf. Der beinahe quadratische Grundriss und die geschwärzten Steine strahlen einen bösartigen Trotz aus, der von den benachbarten Mauern des Calda House weiter angespitzt wird. Weshalb bauen Menschen hier, in einer baumlosen Endlosigkeit, am gefühlten Ende der Welt, eine Burg und ein Herrenhaus? Schutz gegen wen? Herr über was? Die alte, jahrhundertelange Abgeschlossenheit Schottlands scheint für ein paar Augenblicke, während wir zaghaft um die Ruinen trotten, Gestalt zu gewinnen. Für das Universum Schottland ist dieser Ort

nudges his way through the crowd and with a smirk piles his plate high with the darkbrown crumbly curd. "Oh, great," grins one onlooker, "he won't finish his plate and so the sun won't shine..."

Judging by the late summer weather with blue skies and fluffy clouds on the first 30 miles from Ullapool to Unapool, it seems that our Scottish friend must have cleaned up his plate. The drive on the "North Coast 500" through the fishing village of Ardmair, on to Knockan Crag and Loch Assynt reveals a special magic: Almost tenderly, the sun caresses the swaying grasses of the valley, the clear air of the North makes the light seem almost translucent. In the distance the reclusive mountain peaks of Cul Mor and Canisp thrust skywards, and this uninhabited otherworldliness culminates in the ruins of Ardvreck Castle: On the shores of Loch Assynt the foreboding ruins jut out on a rocky promontory, the almost square layout and the blackened stonework exude a malevolent defiance, further intensified by the neighbouring walls of Calda House. Why would people build a castle here in this treeless endlessness at what feels like the

Immer wieder muss die Straße auch durch den Fels getrieben werden, das Innere der Erde tritt rötlich oder glänzend schwarz zutage, Wasser-Rinnsale sickern aus dem bizarr aufgefalteten Gestein, und gleich danach fliegt das Asphaltband wieder auf einem aufgeschütteten Damm über einen dunkelgrünen Loch.

Again and again the road forces its way through the rocks, the interior of the earth appears reddish or shiny black, watercourses, or burns as they're called in Scotland, trickle out of bizarrely-rumpled rock formations and shortly afterwards the asphalt road seems to hover on a man-made dam over a deep green loch.

aber nicht im Nirgendwo, sondern Knotenpunkt eines traditionellen Koordinatensystems. Hinter dem Sichtbaren verbirgt sich Unsichtbares. Schweigend rollen wir weiter über die A894 nach Norden, hinter Unapool über die moderne Kylesku-Brücke und dann weiter durch ein zerfurchtes Land, aus dem sich unzählige Flüsse und Lochs nach Westen in den Atlantik entwässern. Mittlerweile ist auch eine Baumvegetation zurückgekehrt; die ständig im felsigen Gelände neben der Straße vorüberhuschenden Nadelbäume verleihen der Gegend eine beinahe skandinavische Anmutung. Immer wieder muss die Straße auch durch den Fels getrieben werden, das Innere der Erde tritt rötlich oder glänzend schwarz zutage, Wasser-Rinnsale sickern aus dem bizarr aufgefalteten Gestein und gleich danach fliegt das Asphaltband wieder auf einem aufgeschütteten Damm über einen dunkelgrünen Loch. Erst in Scourie findet die Einsamkeit ein vorübergehendes Ende: Zwischen sorgfältig errichteten Steinmäuerchen ducken sich weiße Häuser mit sattgrünen Rasenflächen an die Scourie Bay, die kleine Tankstelle hat tatsächlich geöffnet. Danach gibt es Fish and Chips, und wir tauchen ein in die warme, zarte Köstlichkeit frisch gebackenen Fischs, lecken uns noch lange danach das Salz von den Fingern.

Rund sechs Meilen nach Scourie steuern wir über die Laxford Bridge. Beim Blick in

end of the world? Protection against whom? Lord over what? For a few moments, the old, century-long insularity of Scotland is palpable as we scamper tentatively around the ruins. For the Scottish universe, this place is not in the middle of nowhere, instead it's a hub of a traditional system of coordinates. Behind the visible hides the invisible. Deep in thought, we continue further north on the A894, drive across the modern Kylesku Bridge after Unapool and then on through a rugged countryside from which a myriad of rivers and lochs drain into the Atlantic Ocean. In the meantime, vegetation has returned, pines nestled in the rocky landscape swish past, lending the area an almost Scandinavian feel. Again and again the road forces its way through the rocks, the interior of the earth appears reddish or shiny black, watercourses, or burns as they're called in Scotland, trickle out of bizarrely-rumpled rock formations and shortly afterwards the asphalt road seems to hover on a man-made dam over a deep green loch. Only in Scourie does the wildness come to a temporary end. At Scourie Bay, white houses with lush lawns huddle behind carefully built stone walls, even the tiny gas station is open. Next on the menu, fish and chips. We dive into the warm, delicious freshly-fried fish and lick our salty fingers for a long time afterwards.

About six miles out of Scourie we reach Laxford Bridge. Looking into the babbling, clear

Beinahe eine halbe Stunde lang, rund 14 Meilen weit, fahren wir monoton geradeaus durch ein Tal, das an die Gebirgstäler Montanas erinnert.

For almost half an hour, around 14 miles, we drive in a monotonous straight line through a valley that resembles the mountains of Montana.

den lebhaften Fluss, der sich hier in die Laxford-Bucht ergießt, taucht die Frage nach der Namensgebung überhaupt nicht auf. Rhiconich behütet das Ostende des Loch Inchard, und spätestens hier beginnt unser Run auf das nördliche Ende Schottlands: Beinahe eine halbe Stunde lang, rund 14 Meilen weit, fahren wir monoton geradeaus durch ein Tal, das an die Gebirgstäler Montanas erinnert. Weit entfernte Berge, dazwischen geschwungene Hänge und eine Straße, die wie mit dem Lineal gezogen nach Nordosten pfeilt. In Durness finden wir einen kleinen Kiesplatz neben der Straße am Meer, ein schmaler Pfad führt hier hinunter zum Strand. Feiner Sand zwischen Felsblöcken und ein weites, kaltes Meer. Man könnte noch nach John o' Groats fahren oder in Thurso gar die Fähre nach Stromness nehmen, um wirklich ganz im Norden gewesen zu sein – aber das ist jetzt akademisch.

Eindrücklich bleiben auf den über 100 Meilen nach Inverness die Überquerungen des Kyle of Tongue und viel weiter südlich der Cromarty Firth auf niedrigen Pollerbrücken, die einen beinahe in Kieselsteinmanier über die Wasseroberfläche fliegen lassen. Dann segelt unser Auto in schwindelnder Höhe über die inzwischen vierspurige Hängeseilbrücke am Moray Firth nach Inverness und direkt zu Urquhart, der uns mit entspannter Miene zu einem dunkel leuchtendem Ale den schottischen Klassiker „Haggis, Neeps and Tatties" serviert. Oder auch: Kartoffelbrei mit Steckrüben, einer leichten Whisky-Soße und eben dem Haggis. Ganz ohne den Schafsmagen ähnelt die Füllung aus Nierenfett, Lunge, Leber, Zwiebeln und aufgequollenem Hafermehl auf appetitliche Weise regulärem Hackfleisch, die Konsistenz ist ebenso anregend wie der Duft – einen leeren Teller später hat das Ungeheuer seinen Schrecken verloren. Lecker.

river that flows here into the Laxford Bay, it's clear that the name is derived from the Norse for "salmon fjord." Rhiconich guards the east end of Loch Inchard and this marks the point where our final run to the northern tip of Scotland begins: For almost half an hour, around 14 miles, we drive in a monotonous straight line through a valley that resembles the mountains of Montana. Distant massifs interspersed with gentle slopes and a road that stretches like a ruler to the northeast. In Durness we pull into a small gravel area near the sea. A narrow path leads down to the beach with fine sand between boulders and an expansive, chilly ocean. One could drive on to John o' Groats or take the ferry in Thurso to Stromness to really experience the very northern tip – but this is now academic.

The 100 or so miles to Inverness are just as impressive. The crossings of the Kyle of Tongue and much further south of the Cromarty Firth over low bollard bridges allow us to almost skip like pebbles on the surface of the water. Our car then sails at dizzy heights over the now four-lane suspension bridge at the Moray Firth to Inverness and directly to Urquhart, where we treat ourselves (with neutral expressions) to a dark ale served with the Scottish classic "haggis, neeps and tatties" or mashed potatoes with turnips, a light whisky sauce and…well…haggis. Without the sheep's stomach, the filling of suet, lungs, liver, onions and stock-soaked oatmeal looks a little like ground beef, the consistency is as appetising as the aroma – an empty plate later and the beast has lost its horror. Delicious.

ULLAPOOL INVERNESS

Die Westküste des schottischen Festlands ähnelt mit ihren tief ins Land geschnittenen Buchten und Fjords, den Bergen und der geröllbedeckten Landschaft an vielen Stellen ihrer skandinavischen Nachbarschaft im Osten. Dass die frühe Geschichte Schottlands darüber hinaus immer wieder durch Besiedlung aus Skandinavien geprägt wurde, ist an vielen Ortsnamen und regionalen Geschichten abzulesen – es macht große Freude, bei der Fahrt zum nördlichen Ende Großbritanniens diese Ahnungen und Andeutungen einzusammeln. Von Ullapool aus entfernen wir uns aber zuerst vom Atlantik und fahren bis Unapool durchs Inland. Dann folgen wir der Küstenlinie bis Scourie und ziehen dort eine Gerade nach Durness an der Nordküste. Von hier aus geht es einige Meilen in Richtung Osten, dann beginnt der lange Weg über die Südspitze des Loch Shin bis nach Inverness, der eindeutig größten Stadt des nördlichen Schottland.

—

Many places along the west coast of the Scottish mainland, with its bays and fjords cutting deep inland and scree-sloped mountains, resemble its Scandinavian neighbours in the east. Indeed, the early history of Scotland has always been characterised by settlers from Scandinavia and this can be seen by the many local names and regional stories. It's a great joy to drive to the northern tip of Great Britain and learn about these morsels. From Ullapool we say goodbye for the time being to the Atlantic. We pop inland to Unapool and out again along the coastline to Scourie. From there it's straight ahead to Durness and the north coast. We drive several miles to the east from here before beginning the long journey over the southern tip of Loch Shin to Inverness, definitely the largest city in northern Scotland.

310 KM • CA. 5 STUNDEN // 193 MILES • 5 HOURS

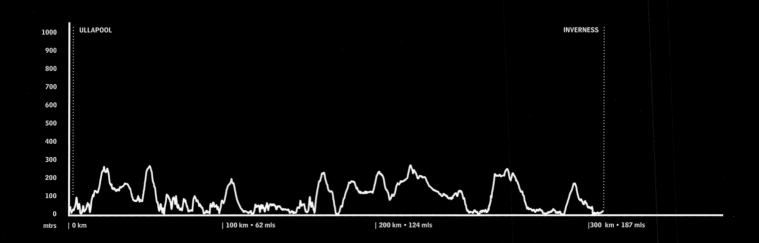

INVERNESS EDINBURGH

523 KM · CA. 8 STUNDEN // 325 MILES · APP. 8 HOURS

Letzte Etappe, frühes Aufstehen – mit den ersten Sonnenstrahlen verlassen wir Inverness über die A96 nach Osten. Am Flughafen, wenige Meilen von der Stadt entfernt, wartet Ian mit seinem Helikopter. Den Breakfast Tea gibt es jetzt im Crew-Raum, während unser Pilot seine Flugvorbereitungen trifft.

—

For our final leg we're up at the crack of dawn and heading east out of Inverness on the A96. At the airport a few miles out of the city, Ian waits for us with his helicopter. We drink our breakfast tea in the crew room while our pilot completes his preflight preparations.

HOTELS & RESTAURANT

MONACHYLE MHOR HOTEL
BALQUHIDDER, LOCHEARNHEAD,
PERTHSHIRE, FK19 8PQ
TEL: +44 1877 384622
WWW. MHOR.NET

MHOR 84 MOTEL
BALQUHIDDER, LOCHEARNHEAD,
PERTHSHIRE, FK19 8NY.
TEL: +44 1877 384 646
WWW. MHOR.NET

Die CURVES-Crew hat die Welt schon öfter aus der Vogelperspektive gesehen, aber irgendwie haben heute alle das Gefühl, etwas ganz Besonderes zu erleben: Schottland von oben.

Mit dem Hubschrauber dürfte es kein Problem sein, in wenigen Minuten eine Strecke zurückzulegen, für die wir im Auto viele Stunden gebraucht haben. Einfach von Tal zu Tal, rüber nach Applecross, runter zur Isle of Skye, dann weiter nach Glencoe und vielleicht sogar bis Loch Lomond. Kurz nach zehn Uhr dreht die Maschine auf, Ian wirft den Helikopter über den Firth, hinter uns wird Inverness immer kleiner. Das Land unter uns ist zuerst grün und der Himmel von glasigem, kaltem Licht erfüllt, dann plötzlich sind wir über einem glühenden Planet in Ocker-Orange angekommen. Ians Stimme knirscht in den Kopfhörern gegen das Hämmern der Rotoren und die brüllend singende Turbine an, immer wieder ist auf dem Grund tief unten der dahinhuschende Schatten des Hubschraubers zu sehen. Und dann fliegen wir in die unverwechselbare Bergflanke des Applecross-Passes, sofort zu erkennen am runden Kegel des linken Gipfels. Im Helikopter schweigt alles, andächtig schauen wir auf den leuchtend blauen Loch Kishorn hinunter, in dessen klarem Wasser die runden Netzgehege der Lachszüchter hier und dort kleine Strukturen bilden. Das saftig grüne Tal des River Kishorn leuchtet in der Sonne, die Berge auf der anderen Seite des Loch scheinen fast schwarz, aber hier, auf unserer Seite, lodern die Flanken des Bealach na Bà im intensiven Morgenlicht intensiv golden. Ian treibt den Helikopter nur wenige Meter über der Passhöhe in den steil abfallenden Trichter hinunter zum Loch, schlagartig sackt der Erdboden unter uns weg.

Dann hämmert die Maschine auch in Richtung Fort William. Das Wetter hier im Landesinneren zieht langsam zu, schwere Regenwolken schieben sich zwischen die

The CURVES crew is no stranger to viewing the world from a bird's eye perspective, but somehow today we have the feeling we're going to experience something very special: Scotland from above, it shouldn't be a problem to cover the distance that took us many hours in the car in just a few minutes with a helicopter. Simply jounce from valley to valley, over to Applecross, down to the Isle of Skye, then on to Glencoe and possibly even Loch Lomond.

Just after ten o'clock the blades begin to whir, Ian banks the helicopter over the Firth, Inverness fades into the distance behind us. At first, the countryside below is green, the sky filled with a translucent, cold light. Suddenly we reach a glowing planet of ochre-orange. Ian's voice crackles through the headset against the thwack of the rotors and the shrill howl of the turbine. Far below, the chopper's shadow races us. As we fly between the incomparable mountain flanks of Applecross Pass, we immediately recognise the rounded cone of the left peak. All goes silent inside the helicopter. Awestruck, we gaze down at the bright blue of Loch Kishorn, round net cages of salmon farmers form small structures here and there in its clear water. The lush green valley of the River Kishorn glistens in the sun, the mountains on the other side of the loch seem almost black, but here, on our side, the flanks of Bealach na Bà blaze golden in the intensive morning light. Ian sweeps mere metres over the top of the pass and suddenly the ground drops away beneath us into the steep funnel down to the loch.

The chopper thumps on towards Fort William. The weather here inland starts to close in, dark rain clouds gather between the mountain giants, summits disappear and the valleys are plunged into a pale twilight. A smattering of sun rays pierce through the clouds to the earth creating a mystical aura. Today, Glencoe could be the landscape star of a bloody, mysterious

Das Land unter uns ist zuerst grün und der Himmel von glasigem, kaltem Licht erfüllt, dann plötzlich sind wir über einem glühenden Planet in Ocker-Orange angekommen.

At first, the countryside below is green, the sky filled with a translucent, cold light. Suddenly we reach a glowing planet of ochre-orange.

Bergriesen, verbergen Gipfel und tauchen die Täler in ein fahles Zwielicht. Nur vereinzelt dringen Sonnenstrahlen bis zur Erde durch, eine mystische Aura bildend – Glencoe könnte heute der Landschafts-Star eines blutigen, athmosphärischen Wikinger-Thrillers sein. Ian drückt in dieser geradezu magischen Landschaft den Helikopter weit hinunter und wir fegen kaum hundert Meter über dem Rannoch Moor entlang der A82. Dann haben wir den südlichsten Punkt unseres Flugs erreicht, in einem großen Bogen zirkelt die Maschine nach Norden, Kurs Inverness. Wir schlingern in den Fallwinden der sich tief unter uns ausbreitenden Täler, hüpfen dann wieder so dicht über die Kämme der Bergketten, dass die Rotorblätter beinahe die Bergflanken rasieren.

Als der Hubschrauber im freundlichen Sonnenschein der lieblichen Welt von Inverness landet, ist das kaum zu fassen. Wir schütteln einem grinsenden Ian die Pranke, taumeln dann erschüttert zum Auto und bekommen auf den ersten Kilometern kaum ein Wort heraus. Vor unserem inneren Auge huschen immer noch die hunderte kleinen Tümpel und Lochs vorüber, die sich in den Senken der Berge verstecken und die man von der Straße im Tal aus niemals sieht. Die Highlands sind aus Wasser gemacht, das sich sammelt, den Boden und das Moor tränkt, fließend und sickernd. Als letzte Erinnerung bleibt die Farbe, eine vollkommen monochromatische und dennoch magisch vielseitige Dauer-Explosion von Orangebraun. Die milde Küste östlich von Inverness, die mit ihren flachen Ebenen

Viking thriller. Ian pushes the helicopter far down into this almost magical landscape and we sweep not even a hundred metres above the Rannoch Moor along the A82. We've reached the southernmost point of the flight. In a large arc, the helicopter circles north on course for Inverness. We lurch in the mountain-valley winds which flow down the slopes and gather in the deep valleys below. Again, we bounce over the mountain crest, the rotor blades almost shaving the mountain flanks.

When the helicopter lands back in the warm sunshine of lovely Inverness it's hard to believe. We shake a grinning Ian's hand, stagger to the car shaken and can barely speak a word for the first few kilometres. In our mind's eye, we're still seeing hundreds of tarns and lochs swishing under us to the left and right, hidden in the mountain troughs, which no one ever sees from the road through the valley. The Highlands are made of water that collects, soaks the soil and the moors, flowing and seeping. A final memory is of the colours, a complete monochrome yet still a magically diverse, nonstop explosion of oranges and browns. The mild coast to the east of Inverness, which looks almost like France or the South of England with its flat plains, makes

Über die Spey-Brücke, dann auf die A939 bis Bridge of Brown ins Malt Whisky-Land. Wir durchqueren Tomintoul und treiben über die Lecht Road immer weiter ins obere Stockwerk der Hügel, während ringsum das Heidekraut blüht.

Over the Spey bridge, onto the A939, to the Bridge of Brown and into malt whisky country. We pass Tomintoul and continue on Lecht Road to the upper floor of the hills, surrounded by meadows of heather in full bloom.

HOTELS & RESTAURANT

KILLIEHUNTLY FARMHOUSE & COTTAGE
BY KINGUSSIE, HIGHLAND PH21 1NZ,
TEL: + 44 (0) 1540 661 619
WWW.KILLIEHUNTLY.SCOT

schon beinahe französisch oder südenglisch wirkt, gibt sich alle Mühe, uns ein Lächeln abzuringen, aber wir wollen zurück in die Berge. In Nairn biegen wir nach Süden ab in Richtung Grantown-on-Spey, und als wir dort dann in der Einsamkeit dahinrollen, tauchen plötzlich die Geschichten und Erinnerungen der letzten Etappen auf – wir beginnen ganz selbstverständlich zu sprudeln und zu erzählen. Vom kleinen Seafood-Restaurant gleich hinter Loch Kishorn. Vom Trupp bärtiger Radfahrer, die sich mit grimmiger Miene entlang der furchterregend hypnotisierenden Geraden zum Loch Tulla kämpften. Oder eben von unseren neuen Camper-Freunden. Das alles ist Schottland geworden. Und dann endlich haben wir wieder den Kopf frei für die letzte Etappe: Den Cairngorms Nationalpark. Über die Spey-Brücke, dann auf die A939 bis Bridge of Brown ins Malt Whisky-Land. Wir durchqueren Tomintoul und treiben über die Lecht Road immer weiter ins obere Stockwerk der Hügel, während ringsum das Heidekraut blüht.

Balmoral Castle muss natürlich sein. Wenn man schon am „Scottish Home to the Royal Family" auftaucht, sollte man auch einen Blick hinter die schwarzen Zäune des Anwesens werfen. Man kann schließlich nicht Haggis essen, aber Balmoral Castle auslassen. Das Anwesen ist Großbritannien at it's best – mit großer Ernsthaftigkeit kultivierte Geschichte, unterstützt von einem Schuss vergnüglichem Elitarismus, ausgeführt als architektonische Allmachts-Geste in Granit. Mit seinen Zinnen, Erkern und Türmen sowie dem massigen Hauptturm hinterlässt

every effort to put a smile back on our faces, but we are homesick for the mountains. In Nairn we turn south towards Grantown-on-Spey and as we suddenly drive into the solitude, the stories and memories of the last stages suddenly bubble up and very naturally we begin to chat: about the tiny seafood restaurant near Loch Kishorn, about the pack of bearded cyclists who fought their way with grim expressions along the frighteningly mesmerising straights to Loch Tulla. Or about our new caravan friends. This has been our Scotland. And finally our heads are clear for the final leg: to Cairngorms National Park. Over the Spey bridge, onto the A939, to the Bridge of Brown and into malt whisky country. We pass Tomintoul and continue on Lecht Road to the upper floor of the hills, surrounded by meadows of heather in full bloom.

Balmoral Castle is a must, of course. When you turn up at the "Scottish Home to the Royal Family" you should take a look behind the black fences of the estate. After all, you can't eat haggis and not go and see Balmoral Castle. The estate is Great Britain at its best – with cultivated history of great seriousness, supported by a dram of rather amusing elitism, executed as an architectural expression of omnipotence in granite. With its battlements, bay windows, towers and the bulky main tower, the castle leaves a big impression, and even if the Queen seems not to be in residence, we can only confirm that the team in charge takes care of the place meticulously. Just in case Her Royal Highness should read this: Your Majesty, don't worry, everything's in tip-top order.

das Schloss einen großartigen Eindruck, und auch wenn die Königin gerade abwesend zu sein scheint, können wir nur bestätigen, dass die hinterlassene Mannschaft den Kasten auch dann akribisch pflegt und zelebriert. Nur für den Fall, dass Ihr das hier lesen solltet, Eure Majestät: Keine Sorge, alles top!

Wenige Meilen hinter Balmoral erleben wir das Kontrastprogramm des einfachen Mannes: Bei einer Pause am River Dee beobachten wir einen wild aussehenden Herrn, der gerade sauber ausgenommene Fische auf Stöcke spießt und diese dann in einer Erdgrube aufstellt. Den knurrend-gurgelnd-gedehnten Dialekt verstehen wir kaum, trotzdem ist nach einigem Hin und Her klar, dass diese Art, Fische in einer Grube im Erdboden zu räuchern, eine alte Wikinger-Gepflogenheit ist – und er sie von seinen Vorfahren aus der Gegend um Aberdeen hierher gebracht hat: „Loch graben, Holz rein, frische Fische rein, anzünden, Flachstuch darüber und warten." Die ganze Angelegenheit qualmt furchtbar, aber als wir den fertigen Fisch aus einer anderen Grube sehen, erleiden wir sofortigen Speichel-Einschuss: warmer, beinahe in der Hand zerfallender Räucherfisch mit aus goldener Haut leuchtendem weißem Fleisch ... Wieder so ein unfassbar schottischer Moment: Duftenden Fisch essen, während man am Ufer eines schwarzen Flusses steht, zwischen wilden Nadelbäumen und Moos. Wird so vermutlich nie wieder passieren, sollte also im Langzeitgedächtnis für schlechte Zeiten abgespeichert werden.

Bis Pitlochry folgen wir der A924 und wechseln dann noch einmal nach Norden in Richtung Kingussie, um die Whiskybrennereien im Westen des Nationalparks abzuklappern, dann zieht es uns endgültig zurück nach Süden. Hinter Perth bleibt das Land belebt, die nun vierspurige Straße hat Autobahncharakter, am Ende rollen wir in Edinburgh aus. Nur eine letzte Handlung, bevor wir uns auf den langen Weg durch England und zum Ärmelkanal machen, bleibt jetzt noch: Ab zum Supermarkt, ein paar Dosen Irn-Bru besorgen und dann mit Blick auf die Skyline den Öffner knacken lassen. Zisch, prickel, schüttel. Kinderkaugummi meets Kohlensäure-Hammer. Zu Haggis passt das aber nicht.

Hinter Perth bleibt das Land belebt, die nun vierspurige Straße hat Autobahncharakter, am Ende rollen wir in Edinburgh aus.

After Perth, the countryside becomes animated. The four-lane road is almost like an autobahn, at the end is Edinburgh.

Several miles after Balmoral we experience the contrast programme of the simple man: During a break at the River Dee we see a wild-looking laddie who has just gutted some fish, skewered them on sticks and put them in a pit. His growling-gurgling dialect is difficult to comprehend, but eventually we work out that hot-smoking this species of fish in a pit is an ancient Viking custom, introduced here by his ancestors from the area around Aberdeen. "Dig a hole, wood in, fresh fish in, light it, cover it with hessian and wait." Smoke billows from everywhere, but when we see the cooked fish in the other pit, our mouths instantly start to water: Warm, flaky smoked fish, golden brown on the outside, white and tender on the inside...another incomparable Scottish experience: Eating aromatic fish while standing on the banks of a black river between wild conifers and moss will probably be a once-in-a-lifetime experience and should be saved as long-term memories for hard times.

We follow the A924 to Pitlochry, veer again to the north towards Kingussie and on to visit some whisky distilleries in the west of the National Park before finally heading south again. After Perth, the countryside becomes animated. The four-lane road is almost like an autobahn, at the end is Edinburgh. One final act is left before we tackle the long drive back through England to the English Channel: Off to the supermarket to buy a couple of cans of Irn-Bru: Gazing at the skyline of Edinburgh, we crack open the ring tab. Hiss, fizz, shake. Kids' chewing gum meets soda-geyser. Don't drink it with haggis.

HOTELS & RESTAURANT

NIRA CALEDONIA
6-10 GLOUCESTER PL,
EDINBURGH EH3 6EF
TEL: +44 131 225 2720
WWW.NIRACALEDONIA.COM

INVERNESS EDINBURGH

Dem überaus lieblichen Küstenabschnitt östlich von Inverness mit seinen flachen Sandstränden folgen wir nur für wenige Meilen, dann zieht es uns nach Süden zum 3800 Quadratkilometer großen Cairngorms Nationalpark. Durch den nahezu menschenleeren und erst seit 2003 geschützten Park führen nur wenige Straßen. Das Land rund um die bis über 1300 Meter hohen Grampian Mountains entfaltet einen ganz eigenen Charakter, weitläufig, intensiv und freundlich. Nach einem Besuch im spektakulären Balmoral Castle folgen wir den großen Hauptverkehrsstraßen im Osten Schottlands bis nach Edinburgh. Die schottische Hauptstadt am Firth of Forth mit ihren rund 500 000 Einwohnern ist das Ziel der letzten Etappe und unserer Schottland-Rundfahrt.

—

We only follow the exceptionally picturesque coastal section east of Inverness with its flat sand beaches for a few miles before heading south to the 3,800-square-kilometre Cairngorms National Park. Only a few roads run through the almost uninhabited park, which was only put under protection in 2003. The land around the 1,300-metre-high Grampian Mountains reveals its own character: expansive, intense and welcoming. After a visit to the spectacular Balmoral Castle we follow the major roads to eastern Scotland and on to Edinburgh. The Scottish capital with around half a million inhabitants on the Firth of Forth is the destination of the last leg of our round-trip of Scotland.

523 KM • CA. 8 STUNDEN // 325 MILES • APP. 8 HOURS

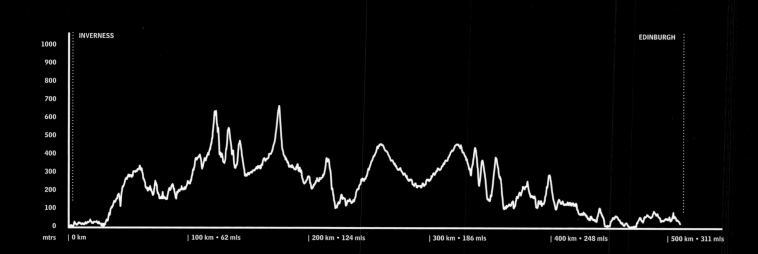

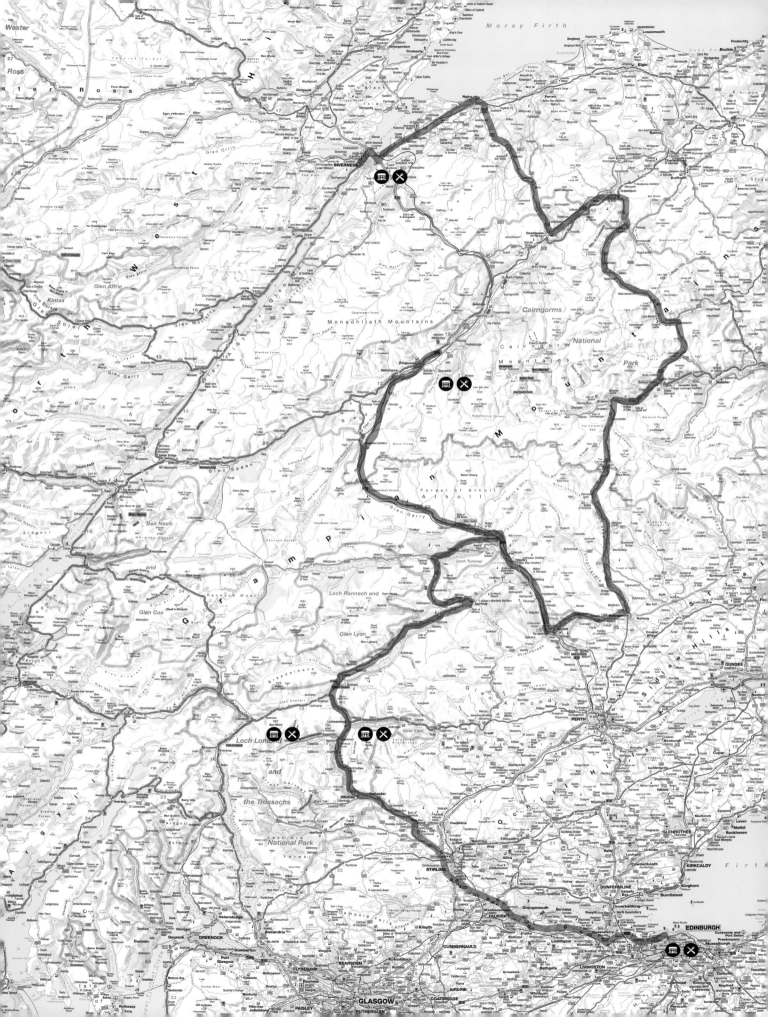

BAC KST AGE

Immer, wenn Europäer mit Fernweh und Reiselust über ihr nächstes Ziel debattieren, taucht ein Phänomen auf: Die Alpen, der Mittelmeer-Raum und vielleicht sogar eine der großen Sehnsuchtsstraßen auf anderen Kontinenten sind längst angefahren und teilweise intensiv aufgesogen worden – aber Schottland fehlt. Es ist ja nicht so, dass der raue Norden der britischen Inseln bei bloßer Namensnennung einen sofortigen Seelen-Burnout und zwanghafte Aufbruchsstimmung verursachen würde, aber es nagt etwas. Es treibt einen um. Eine fast unerklärliche Neugier, die möglicherweise sogar in ihren Grundzügen aus dem Kitsch unzähliger Hollywood-Freiheitskämpfer-Schmonzetten genährt wird oder aus dem Pathos einer diffusen Verehrung für alles Nordische als dem Reservat einer freien, wilden Ursprünglichkeit. Im Endeffekt bleibt das „Woher" dieser Sehnsucht nach Schottland aber auch ganz egal. Wichtiger wird immer mehr das „Wann": Wann kommt man einfach nicht mehr um Schottland herum? Wann ist die Zeit reif? Wann geht es endlich los?

Genau diese Frage haben wir CURVES-Macher uns ebenfalls gestellt, und dass es uns erst in Europas kernigen Nordwesten verschlagen hat, nachdem wir die Alpen und Pyrenäen in

Whenever Europeans with itchy feet and wanderlust consider their next destination, the same phenomenon crops up: The Alps, the Mediterranean, perhaps even one of the great dream road trips on other continents have long been ticked off and some of them enjoyed intensely – but Scotland is missing. Mentioning the rugged north of the British Isles doesn't exactly elicit an overwhelmingly enthusiastic response, but it somehow gnaws. It piques interest. An almost unexplainable curiosity, possibly fed by the kitsch of countless Hollywood freedom fighters or the vague passion for all things Nordic as a bastion of a free, unspoilt wilderness. Ultimately, it doesn't matter "from where" this longing for Scotland comes. More importantly is the "when". When can you no longer ignore Scotland? When is the time ripe? When will it finally happen?

These are the exact questions that we CURVES creators asked, and the fact that we only suggested Europe's rugged northwest after we'd crisscrossed the Alps and the Pyrenees in all directions, after we'd cruised through California and conquered Sicily, is not a judgement, and not a question of priority. Instead, it's perhaps a sign of how unobvious Scotland can be. Other destinations are no more appealing or exciting, but Scotland

allen Himmelsrichtungen durchquert haben, durch Kalifornien gecruist und Sizilien geräubert sind, ist keine Wertung, keine Reihenfolge. Sondern vielleicht auch ein Zeichen dafür, wie wenig naheliegend Schottland sein kann. Andere Destinationen wirken nicht attraktiver oder spannender, aber Schottland ist ein Ziel, um das wir uns tatsächlich lange gedrückt haben, obwohl es immer wieder im Raum stand. Positiv betrachtet, könnte man ja sagen: Wir haben zugesehen, wie sich die Vorfreude langsam aufgebaut hat und dieses herrliche Gefühl intensiv ausgekostet. Gerade vor dem Hintergrund dieser langen, lustvollen Verweigerung war unser Schock nach den ersten Meilen auf schottischen Straßen riesengroß – so unbeschreiblich schön und ergreifend majestätisch hatten wir uns Schottland in keiner Vorbereitungs-Phase vorgestellt. Wenn wir für unsere Panorama-Fotos im Helikopter unterwegs sind, ist eigentlich immer wieder ein gelegentliches „Oh" oder „Ah" zu hören – in Schottland herrschte jedoch atemloses Schweigen. Was für ein verwunschenes Land, was für ein Rausch aus Farben, Dimensionen und Elementen. Wer es hierher geschafft hat, ist tatsächlich privilegiert.

Große Begeisterung haben bei uns aber auch die Menschen Schottlands ausgelöst: Die unkomplizierte, großzügige und entspannte Art der als so raubeinig geschilderten Highlander hat uns sofort gewonnen. Bei aller Robustheit scheinen die Schotten eine ungemein humorvolle, selbstironische und regelrecht poetische Ader zu haben, selbst die banalsten Dinge werden mit einem Augenzwinkern und selbstverständlichem Frohsinn serviert. A propos serviert: Der kulinarische Ruf Schottlands ist bestenfalls zweifelhaft, dass wir hier in den kleinen Seafood-Restaurants aber immer wieder regelrecht hängen geblieben sind, gehört ebenfalls zu den großen Überraschungen unserer Reise. Ein derartiges Gastronomie-Paralleluniversum neben der Straße hätten wir in Italien erwartet, ganz bestimmt aber nicht in Großbritannien. Und wo wir jetzt schon bei Überraschungen sind: Selten hat uns ein Auto während der Produktion von CURVES so sehr zu intensiven Diskussionen angeregt, wie der neue Porsche Panamera 4 E-Hybrid. Nach anfänglicher Zurückhaltung hatte der Hybrid-Sportwagen alle Team-Mitglieder völlig in seinen Bann gezogen. Die begeisternde Mischung aus Porsche-typischen, ansteckend unkomplizierten Vollstrecker-Genen und – ebenso Porsche-typisch – Erste-Klasse-Engineering aus einem technologischen Paralleluniversum macht uns zu Panamera-Fans, der Hybrid ist unser Held. Der Panamera passt ganz großartig zu den Kurven und Kehren der Highlands und sein verblüffend präsentes Fahren trotz sagenhaftem Komfort hat die Tür nach Schottland vielleicht erst richtig weit aufgestoßen.

Und deshalb: Danke! Danke, für die CURVES-Unterstützung durch die Seelenverwandten aus Stuttgart-Zuffenhausen. Danke Panamera. Danke aber auch an alle Freunde und Unterstützer, an all die Windgesichter da draußen, die CURVES zu dem gemacht haben, was es auch nach sieben (größtenteils ausverkauften) Ausgaben immer noch für uns ist: Eine echte Überraschung.

is a place we've been avoiding for a long time, even though it kept cropping up. From a positive point of view one can say: We've observed how the anticipation has gradually increased and the wonderful feeling has been very much savoured. Against the backdrop of this long, much relished denial, our shock after the first miles on Scottish roads was immense: We had never imagined during our preparations just how indescribably beautiful and poignantly majestic Scotland would turn out to be. Whenever we're taking panoramic shots from a helicopter for other projects, we occasionally hear an "Oh" or an "Ah" – but over Scotland there was a breathless silence. What an enchanted world, what a feast of colours, dimensions and elements. Whoever manages to experience this land is truly privileged.

The Scottish folk, too, were reason for great joy. The uncomplicated, generous and relaxed nature of the often brusque-portrayed Highlanders won us over completely. With all their ruggedness, the Scottish people seem to possess an unusually humorous, self-ironic and downright poetic disposition. Even the most banal things are served with a wink and natural good-humour. A propos served: The culinary reputation of Scotland is at best doubtful, but that we kept getting waylaid by little seafood restaurants along the way is also one of the great surprises of our trip. We fully expected such a gastronomic parallel world on Italian roadsides, but certainly not in the United Kingdom. And since we're on the topic on surprises: Rarely has a car induced such deep discussions during the production of CURVES like the new Porsche Panamera 4 E-Hybrid. After initial reserve, the hybrid sports car completely captivated the entire crew. The exciting mix of infectiously straight-forward driving dynamics typical of Porsche and first class engineering – also typically Porsche – from a technological parallel universe turned us into Panamera fans. The hybrid is our hero. The Panamera fits perfectly with the curves and sweeps of the Highlands, and its astonishingly responsive handling combined with outstanding comfort very likely pushed the door to Scotland wide open for us.

So, thank you! Thank you to the kindred spirits from Stuttgart-Zuffenhausen for supporting CURVES. Thank you, Panamera. And thanks, too, to all of our friends and backers, to all the weather-beaten faces out there who have made CURVES what it still is today after seven (mostly sold-out) editions: a real surprise.

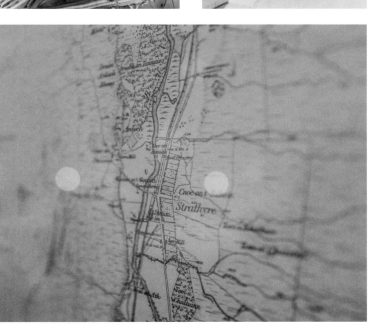

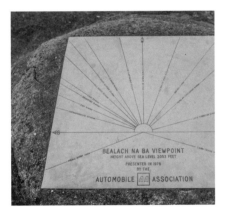

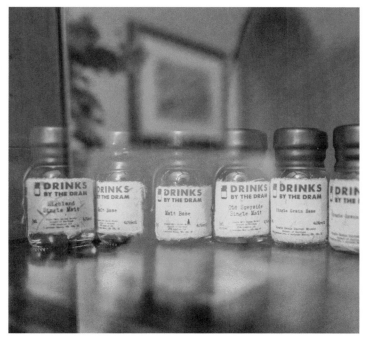

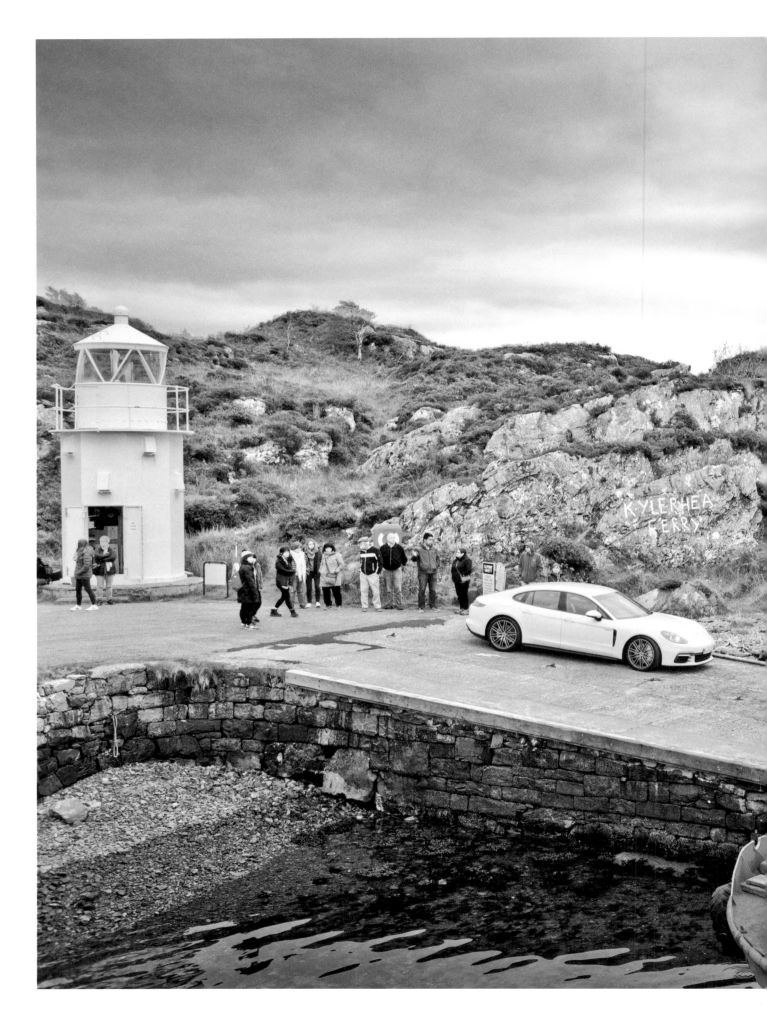

artridges
e larger
soldier's
s" (god

OFFICERS BADGERHEAD SPORRAN worn by a Lieutenant in the Argylls. Although not worn in the trenches it would have been part of his uniform when he was on leave or when he was

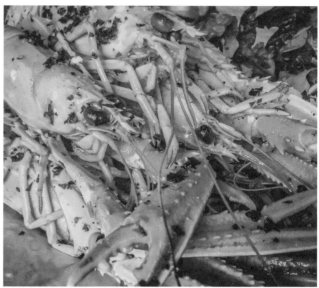

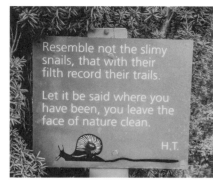

Resemble not the slimy snails, that with their filth record their trails.

Let it be said where you have been, you leave the face of nature clean.

H.T.

Better latte than never.

DANK AN / THANKS TO

MICHAEL DAIMINGER, BEN WINTER, MARCO BRINKMANN, EDWIN BAASKE, DR. STEPHANIE MAIR-HUYDTS, AXEL SCHILDT, SEBASTIAN WAGNER, MICHAEL DORN, ALEXANDER FAILING, MICHAELA BOGNER

SPECIAL FX / SPECIAL FX

ELENA HERRMANN, BASTIAN SCHRAMM, PDG HELICOPTERS

Kraftstoffverbrauch/Emissionen* des Porsche Panamera 4 E-Hybrid / Fuel consumption* Panamera 4 E-Hybrid:

Kraftstoffverbrauch (in l/100 km)*: kombiniert 2,5; CO_2-Emission kombiniert 56 g/km; Stromverbrauch kombiniert 15,9 kWh/100 km.
Fuel consumption (in l/100 km)*: combined 2.5; CO_2 emissions combined 56 g/km; electricity consumption combined 15.9 kWh/100 km.

*Die angegebenen Werte wurden nach dem vorgeschriebenen Messverfahren (§ 2 Nr. 5, 6, 6a Pkw-EnVKV in der jeweils geltenden Fassung) ermittelt.
*Data determined in accordance with the measurement method specified by Section 2 No. 5, 6, 6a of the German Ordinance on the Energy Consumption
  Labelling of Passenger Cars (PkW-EnVKV) in the version currently applicable.

IMPRESSUM / IMPRINT

HERAUSGEBER/
PUBLISHER: CURVES
AINMILLERSTRASSE 25
D-80801 MÜNCHEN

VERANTWORTLICH FÜR
DEN HERAUSGEBER/
RESPONSIBLE FOR
PUBLICATION:
STEFAN BOGNER

KONZEPT/CONCEPT:
STEFAN BOGNER
THIERSCHSTRASSE
D-80538 MÜNCHEN
SB@CURVES-MAGAZIN.COM

DELIUS KLASING
CORPORATE PUBLISHING
SIEKERWALL 21
D-33602 BIELEFELD

REDAKTION/
EDITORIAL CONTENT:
EDWIN BAASKE
MARCO BRINKMANN
STEFAN BOGNER
BEN WINTER

ART DIRECTION, LAYOUT, FOTOS/
ART DIRECTION, LAYOUT, PHOTOS:
STEFAN BOGNER
FOTOS MAKING OF/
PHOTOS MAKING-OF:
MICHAEL DAIMINGER

TEXT/TEXT: BEN WINTER
VORWORT/FOREWORD:
BASTIAN SCHRAMM

MOTIVAUSARBEITUNG
LITHOGRAPHIE/SATZ/
POST-PRODUCTION,
LITHOGRAPHY/SETTING:
MICHAEL DORN

KARTENMATERIAL/MAP MATERIAL:
MAIRDUMONT
MARCO-POLO-STR. 1,
73760 OSTFILDERN (KEMNAT)

ÜBERSETZUNG/TRANSLATION
KAYE MUELLER

PRODUKTIONSLEITUNG/
PRODUCTION MANAGEMENT:
JÖRN HEESE

DRUCK/PRINT:
KUNST- UND WERBEDRUCK
BAD OEYNHAUSEN

2. AUFLAGE/2ND EDITION 2018
ISBN 978-3-667-11397-9

DELIUS KLASING

AUSGEZEICHNET MIT / AWARDED WITH

**DDC GOLD - DEUTSCHER DESIGNER CLUB E.V. FÜR GUTE GESTALTUNG // IF COMMUNICATION DESIGN AWARD 2012
BEST OF CORPORATE PUBLISHING // ADC BRONZE // RED DOT BEST OF THE BEST & D&AD // NOMINIERT FÜR
DEN DEUTSCHEN DESIGNPREIS 2015 // WINNER AUTOMOTIVE BRAND CONTEST 2014 // GOOD DESIGN AWARD 2014**

CURVES AUSGABEN / OTHER ISSUES OF CURVES

PYRENÄEN
PYRENEES
Im Handel erhältlich/Available in stores

ÖSTERREICH
AUSTRIA
Im Handel erhältlich/Available in stores

SCHWEIZ
SWITZERLAND
Im Handel erhältlich/Available in stores

NORDITALIEN
NORTHERN ITALY
Im Handel erhältlich/Available in stores

FRANKREICH
FRANCE
Im Handel erhältlich/Available in stores

USA · KALIFORNIEN
USA · CALIFORNIA
Im Handel erhältlich/Available in stores

SIZILIEN
SICILY
Im Handel erhältlich/Available in stores